"*Do Hard Things* is an extraordinary book. In fact, I believe it will prove to be one of the most life-changing, family-changing, church-changing, and culture-changing books of this generation. I'd love for every teenager to read this book, but I'm just as eager for every parent, church leader, and educator to read it. If you do the hard thing of saying no to distractions and yes to this remarkable book, I guarantee you'll be richly rewarded."

—RANDY ALCORN, best-selling author of *Heaven*
    and *The Treasure Principle*

"Adult expectations for youth are too low. And these twins are out to raise them. Don't adapt to the low cultural expectations for youth. Set high ones. Youth can become examples for adults. Think that way. Dream that way. Or as the Harris brothers would say, 'Rebel against low expectations.' May God give us a vision for the next generation that glorifies the gospel of Christ and leads thousands of young people to the cross, where they find forgiveness of sins, broken-hearted humility, and Christ-exalting courage to rebel against low expectations and do hard things."

—JOHN PIPER, Desiring God Ministries and best-selling
    author of *Don't Waste Your Life*

"*Do Hard Things* is so important. It is challenging teenagers to rebel against the low expectations placed on them, not the least of which are low spiritual expectations. And the voices that are asking teens to rise to meet this challenge are voices from their own generation. That thrills me. If you've got a teenager—or a grandson or granddaughter—I encourage you to pick up a copy of *Do Hard Things*. It would make a great graduation present or summer reading. And don't just give them the book; make a point to ramp up your interaction with the teens God has put in your life. Become a spiritual mentor and help them rebel against low expectations. Help them become rebels with a good cause, seeking more out of life than mindless channel-surfing."

—CHUCK COLSON, founder of Prison Fellowship

and best-selling author of *How Now Shall We Live?*

"Do Hard Things is easy to read, but it will challenge you to the core. It is inspiring, insightful, and practical. Parents, this book will get your teens into the right kind of trouble—the kind that comes when they dream, take risks for God, and dare to flout the status quo. Put it in their hands. Read it yourself. It's never too late to do hard things."

—JOSHUA HARRIS, pastor, author, and older brother

"Alex and Brett Harris are two extraordinary young men with a revolutionary message. In a culture where laziness and ease is often the order of the day for teenagers, *Do Hard Things* presents a radical and provocative alternative. I heartily recommend this book."

—R. ALBERT MOHLER JR., president of Southern Baptist
Theological Seminary

"This book is a refreshing wake-up call to our generation. We *can* do hard things and give ourselves to something huge for the kingdom of God!"

—LEELAND MOORING, Grammy-nominated
recording artist

"This book will create a distinct distaste in your soul for living an easy and comfortable life. I pray that God will use this book to inspire many young people (and old alike!) to do hard things by God's grace for the glory of His name."

—C. J. MAHANEY, Sovereign Grace Ministries, author of *Living the Cross-Centered Life* and *Humility: True Greatness*

"Alex and Brett capture the passion and potential of our generation perfectly in this book. In *Do Hard Things,* they encourage us to go above and beyond the status quo in everything from schoolwork to serving the poor. This is a truly unique and sorely needed book."

—ZACH HUNTER, abolitionist and author of *Be the Change,*
age 16

"*Do Hard Things* is exactly the message our generation needs to hear. This book challenges us to stop and recall the things God has put in our hearts to do and take time to do them *now.* Let's address the low expectations and call our generation to rise up and see what the Lord can do when we do hard things."

—BARLOWGIRL, recording artist

"This is an important book. And not just for those wanting to launch successfully into adulthood, but also for discontented twenty- and thirty-somethings who long to be catapulted into significance. The propositions in this book are neither wishful thinking about what could be nor a wistful reflection on how things used to be. The Harris brothers demonstrate with their lives and through the examples of countercultural dream-big teens around the world that young adults can achieve great things and live rich, intentional, excellent, and meaningful lives."

—TED SLATER, editor of *Boundless,* Focus
on the Family

"Alex and Brett Harris are leading the way for the fight to save their generation, and in *Do Hard Things* they are beckoning others to join them. I pray that teenagers will listen to their cry and join them on the front lines."

—RON LUCE, founder of Teen Mania Ministries
and author of *Battle Cry for a Generation*

"If you are a young person who wants to affect this world for Jesus Christ, read this book! I have watched Alex and Brett take on new and daunting endeavors with resolve and determination and, as a result, mature and develop into leaders for this generation and an example for *all* generations of reaching to fulfill your full potential in and for Christ."

—JUSTICE TOM PARKER, Alabama Supreme Court

"Alex and Brett are the real deal, and *Do Hard Things* is a real wake-up call not just for young people but for all God's people. I can't recommend it highly enough."

—SHANNON ETHRIDGE, best-selling author of *Every Young Woman's Battle* and *Completely His*

"Add years to your life! This book is a how-to guide for recovering the years thirteen to nineteen. It's a good read—the trap of low expectations, the danger of leisure, surprising stories—this is stirring stuff! *Do Hard Things* is a winning combination of optimism and challenge."

—MARK DEVER, pastor of Capitol Hill Baptist Church and founder of 9Marks.org

"*Do Hard Things* is the textbook for anyone who works with teens; it's a philosophical and foundational must-read."

—TIMOTHY ELDRED, executive director of Christian Endeavor International

"As a university professor, I am well aware of the Gen Y propensity to demand more recognition for less effort and to associate self-esteem with mere being rather than for actual accomplishment. *Do Hard Things* is a call to teenagers everywhere to channel their energy into world-changing activity with eternal significance. I highly recommend it."

—DR. ALEX CHEDIAK, associate professor of engineering at California Baptist University and author of *With One Voice*

"Our generation is filled with apathetic, complacent, and immature wimps. By contrast, Brett and Alex are leaders in our generation, and their message is that you can be too."

—Hans Zeiger, author of *Reagan's Children* and *Get Off My Honor*

"The simple title, *Do Hard Things,* in one sense summarizes the high-energy, cheerleader-like optimism of the book's pages. Just do it! Do it! Do it! The argument is buttressed with stories and anecdotes to encourage the faint-hearted. But this book's foundations are much, much deeper. By their words and by their example, the Harris twins are provoking Christian teenagers to raise their sights. If I have any reservations about Alex and Brett's book, such doubts are less about them and more about the readiness of the evangelical culture to hear and respond to such a heady, serious challenge. But that, of course, is exactly what this is all about—a couple of nineteen-year-olds, wise beyond their years, asking the rest of us to do hard things."

—Joel Belz, founder of *World Magazine*

To read endorsements from real teens, parents, and youth workers, visit TheRebelution.com

A TEENAGE
REBELLION
AGAINST
LOW EXPECTATIONS

DOHARDTHINGS

ALEX&BRETT HARRIS

MULTNOMAH
BOOKS

Do Hard Things
Published by Multnomah Books
12265 Oracle Boulevard, Suite 200
Colorado Springs, CO 80921

Trade Paperback ISBN 978-1-60142-829-5
Hardcover ISBN 978-1-60142-112-8
eBook ISBN 978-1-60142-161-6

Published in the United States by WaterBrook Multnomah, an imprint of the Crown
Publishing Group, a division of Penguin Random House LLC, New York.

MULTNOMAH® and its mountain colophon are registered trademarks of Penguin
Random House LLC.

The Library of Congress has cataloged the hardcover edition as follows:
Harris, Alex, 1988–
    Do hard things : a teenage rebellion against low expectations / by Alex and Brett
Harris. — 1st ed.
        p. cm.
    Includes bibliographical references.
    ISBN 978-1-60142-112-8
    1. Self-actualization (Psychology)—Religious aspects—Christianity. 2. Self-actualization
(Psychology) in adolescence. 3. Expectation—Religious aspects—Christianity. 4. Adoles-
cent psychology. I. Harris, Brett, 1988– II. Title.
    BV4598.2.H36 2008
    248.8'3—dc22

                                                    2008006226

Printed in the United States of America
2016

10 9 8 7 6 5 4 3

SPECIAL SALES
Most WaterBrook Multnomah books are available in special quantity discounts when
purchased in bulk by corporations, organizations, and special interest groups. Custom
imprinting or excerpting can also be done to fit special needs. For information, please
e-mail SpecialMarkets@WaterBrookMultnomah.com or call 1-800-603-7051.

To our parents, Gregg and Sono Harris.
This book is the message of your lives.
Our triumph is your triumph. We love you.

CONTENTS

PART 3
JOIN THE REBELUTION

FOREWORD
BY CHUCK NORRIS

As a young man, I discovered the power of doing hard things. Abject poverty, a father's alcoholism and desertion of our family, and my own shyness were a few of the obstacles I faced and overcame growing up. My mother always told me, "God has a plan for your life." And she's right. Each of us is called to reach for greatness. There really is a hero in all of us. We've all been designed by God to be a blessing to many—a hero to some.

But there's only one way to get there—it's described by the title of this book: *Do Hard Things*.

Today we live in a culture that promotes comfort, not challenges. Everything is about finding ways to escape hardship, avoid pain, and dodge duty. In the past, young people were expected to make significant contributions to society. Today, our culture expects very little from teens—not much more than staying in school and doing a few chores. A sad consequence of such low expectations is that life-changing lessons go unlearned.

To whom can we turn to motivate a new generation of giants? I've found the answer. Alex and Brett Harris and their book, *Do Hard Things*.

I know the twins personally and can vouch for their integrity and wisdom. I've seen their passion to raise up a new generation of tough-spirited young people. They are amazing young men, uniquely qualified to inspire others to reach for great things.

One of my life's principles is to develop myself to the maximum of my potential in all ways and to help others do the same. Brett and Alex come straight from the same mold, but with an even greater potential to reach young people around the world.

Their book is far more than a typical how-to book. From an insightful historical overview of the teen years to personal plans for helping teens hurdle tough obstacles, the authors sound a battle cry to raise the cultural bar on teenage potential and to challenge young people to reach for their God-given best.

Do Hard Things will help recruit, develop, and deploy a new generation of young culture warriors. With God's help, the book you're holding will usher in an era in which it can once again be said of our youth, "I write to you, *young men,* because you are strong, and the word of God abides in you, and you have overcome the evil one" (1 John 2:14).

Start reading now. Then do hard things!

—Chuck Norris
www.chucknorris.com

LOOKING BACK, LOOKING AHEAD

Only yesterday, it seems, two teenage brothers got excited about a big idea that young people were being underestimated—badly, and with devastating consequences. What made it worse, the brothers believed, was that a whole generation of teens had bought into a culture of low expectations. Kids everywhere were essentially being groomed for failure before they had ever been tested for success. Before they'd ever been invited to set their minds, wills, and hearts on making a mark for God in the world.

How tragic!

And history showed it didn't have to be that way. History showed, in fact, that the teen years were meant to be a season of daring, of high hopes and real achievements, a one-time-only opportunity for a guy or girl to set a course for a truly remarkable life.

The brothers—okay, that would be us, Alex and Brett—came up with a plan to change all that, then invited other young people and their parents to join in. And that was the beginning of the Rebelution.

What a difference five years have made! What started as a blog (TheRebelution.com) became a best-selling book, *Do Hard Things,* which led to youth conferences around the country every summer. And all of that, by God's grace and a lot of hard work, had spawned an international youth movement with this red book as its manifesto.

To date, *Do Hard Things* has been translated into over a dozen languages, including French, Korean, Czech, and Portuguese, sparking sister campaigns in Europe, Asia, and South America. Young people from New York to Los Angeles, from São Paulo to Manila, are rebelling against low expectations for the glory of God.

"Regards from snowy Poland," reads a recent e-mail from sisters Kornelia and Eunika Chojeckie. They wrote to say they had just finished a "do hard things" presentation in Lublin.

The Chojeckie sisters are two of the founding members of a Rebelution-inspired youth campaign spreading across

Eastern Europe. They're sponsoring events and a growing, multilingual social networking site with users from Poland, Hungary, Bosnia and Herzegovina, Moldova, and Kazakhstan.

Here in the United States, rebelutionaries have raised hundreds of thousands of dollars for missions and charity, won prestigious film festivals, earned Grammy Award nominations, fought human trafficking around the world, and been invited to speak at the White House on multiple occasions.

"Do hard things" is slowly entering the national consciousness, making cameo appearances in *ESPN The Magazine*, nationally syndicated comic strips, blockbuster feature films, as well as in the speeches of major political leaders from Senator John McCain to President Barack Obama.

But the true engine of the Rebelution has been the steady, long-term faithfulness of thousands of young people you've never heard of, quietly stepping outside their comfort zones, going beyond what is expected or required, investing their teenage and college years in undertakings of real and lasting consequence, and never backing down from hard things worth doing.

Across the globe—from Parisian neighborhoods to Ivy League classrooms—a generation of rebels is rising through steady, one-foot-after-the-other, daily obedience to Jesus Christ. This is a quiet, worldwide revolution, and you're invited. Our mantra is "do hard things," and our mission statement is 1 Timothy 4:12, "Don't let anyone look down on you because you are young, but set an example for the believers in speech, in life, in love, in faith and in purity" (NIV).

We were eighteen when we wrote *Do Hard Things*. Since then we've been able to travel and speak in dozens of major cities in the United States, Canada, Switzerland, and Japan—reaching hundreds of thousands of teens, parents, and youth workers through live events and media appearances. We've been able to preach the gospel to our generation and seen thousands of bold professions of faith in Jesus Christ. We've written another book called *Start Here,* a field guide for putting the "do hard things" mind-set into practice.

We attended and graduated from college (Patrick Henry College, Purcellville, Virginia), becoming the first in our immediate family to do so. We watched our mother bravely battle cancer and go to be with Jesus on July 4, 2010. We've fought our own personal battles against sin, wrestled through questions of calling, and for long stretches of time, stepped out of the limelight to just practice what we preach.

And we both got married—Alex to Courtney, and Brett to Ana. All together, the last five years have been the most significant and challenging years of our lives. We've been stretched, pushed, and strengthened. We haven't backed down, and we haven't let up. It's been hard—and it's been good.

Which brings us to the fifth anniversary edition you're holding. When WaterBrook Multnomah approached us about an update, we were faced with some important questions: How do you update something without changing it? How do you offer something new without compromising what made the old so effective?

In the end, we opted for a conservative approach, leaving the original content untouched while adding new material as appendixes. It's the same book, but better. And whether you're a first-time reader or a long-time rebelutionary, we think you'll really like it.

This new content begins with "Questions (and Stories) to Get You Started," which delves into the queries we hear most often:

- "I'm ready to get started—on *something*! What should I do now?"
- "Do small hard things really count?"

Next you'll find the list "100 Hard Things" to get your own creative juices flowing. These are real-life examples of hard things young people just like you have done—from making care packages for members of the military, to starting an after-school Bible study, to training for and running a marathon.

Finally, we've included a *Do Hard Things* study guide for personal or group use, along with information about downloadable video resources we created with LifeChurch.tv.

We think you'll find these new tools helpful and encouraging as you champion the vision of teenage *high* expectations in your area and apply your heart, mind, and strength to the adventure ahead.

G. K. Chesterton once wrote, "The Christian ideal has not been tried and found wanting. It has been found difficult; and left untried." Our hope and prayer is that you would join us in doing hard things, that together we would be *the* generation of Christian young people who find it difficult to follow hard after Christ...and yet still try.

Together for His glory,

Alex and Brett Harris

PART 1

RETHINKING THE TEEN YEARS

MOST PEOPLE DON'T

A different kind of teen book

Most people don't expect you to understand what we're going to tell you in this book. And even if you understand, they don't expect you to care. And even if you care, they don't expect you to do anything about it. And even if you do something about it, they don't expect it to last.

Well, we do.

This is a different kind of teen book. Check online or walk through your local bookstore. You'll find plenty of books written by fortysomethings who, like, totally understand what it's like being a teenager. You'll find a lot of cheap throwaway books for teens because young people today aren't supposed to care about books or see any reason to keep them around. And you'll find a wide selection of books where you never have to read anything twice—because the message is dumbed-down. Like, just for you.

What you're holding in your hands right now is a challenging book *for* teens *by* teens who believe our generation is ready for a change. Ready for something that doesn't promise a whole new life if you'll just buy the right pair of jeans or use the right kind of deodorant. We believe our generation is ready to rethink what teens are capable of doing and becoming. And we've noticed that once wrong ideas are debunked and cleared away, our generation is quick to choose a better way, even if it's also more difficult.

We're nineteen-year-old twin brothers, born and raised in Oregon, taught at home by our parents, and striving to follow Christ as best we can. We've made more than our share of mistakes. And although we don't think "average teenagers" exist, there is nothing all that extraordinary about us personally.

Still, we've had some extraordinary experiences. At age sixteen, we interned at the Alabama Supreme Court. At seventeen, we served as grass-roots directors for four statewide political campaigns. At eighteen, we authored the most popular Christian teen blog on the web. We've been able to speak to thousands of teens and their parents at conferences in the United States and internationally and to reach millions online. But if our teen years have been different than most, it's not because we're somehow better than other teens, but because we've been motivated by a simple but very big idea. It's an idea you're going to encounter for yourself in the pages ahead.

We've seen this idea transform "average" teenagers into world-changers able to accomplish incredible things. And they started by simply being willing to break the mold of what society thinks teens are capable of.

So even though the story starts with us, this book really isn't about us, and we would never want it to be. It's about something God is doing in the hearts and minds of our generation. It's about an idea. It's about rebelling against low expectations. It's about a movement that is changing the attitudes and actions of teens around the world. And we want you to be part of it.

This book invites you to explore some radical questions:

- Is it possible that even though teens today have more freedom than any other generation in history, we're actually missing out on some of the best years of our lives?

- Is it possible that what our culture says about the purpose and potential of the teen years is a lie and that we are its victims?

- Is it possible that our teen years give us a once-in-a-lifetime opportunity for huge accomplishments—as individuals and as a generation?
- And finally, what would our lives look like if we set out on a different path entirely—a path that required more effort but promised a lot more reward?

We describe that alternative path with three simple words: "do hard things."

If you're like most people, your first reaction to the phrase "do hard things" runs along the lines of, "Hard? Uh-oh. Guys, I just remembered that I'm supposed to be somewhere else. Like, right now."

We understand this reaction. It reminds us of a story we like to tell about a group of monks. Yep, monks.

On the outskirts of a small town in Germany is the imaginary abbey of Dundelhoff. This small stone monastery is home to a particularly strict sect of Dundress monks, who have each vowed to live a life of continual self-denial and discomfort.

Instead of wearing comfy T-shirts and well-worn jeans like most people, these monks wear either itchy shirts made from goat hair or cold chain mail worn directly over bare skin. Instead of soft mattresses, pillows, and warm blankets, they sleep on the cold stone floors of the abbey. You might have read somewhere that monks are fabulous cooks? Well, not these monks. They eat colorless, tasteless sludge—once a day. They only drink lukewarm water.

We could go on, but you get the picture. No matter what decision they face, Dundress monks always choose the more difficult option, the one that provides the least physical comfort, holds the least appeal, offers the least fun. Why? Because they believe that the more miserable they are, the holier they are; and the holier they are, the happier God is.

So these miserable monks must be poster boys for "do hard things." Right?

Wrong!

We're not plotting to make your life miserable. We're not recommending that you do any and every difficult thing. For example, we're not telling you to rob a bank, jump off a cliff, climb Half Dome with your bare hands, or stand on your head for twenty-four hours straight. We are not telling you to do pointless (or stupid) hard things just because they're hard. And if you're a Christian, we're certainly not telling you that if you work harder or make yourself uncomfortable on purpose, God will love you more. He will never—could never—love you any more than He does right now.

So that's what we're not doing. What we *are* doing is challenging you to grab hold of a more exciting option for your teen years than the one portrayed as normal in society today. This option has somehow gotten lost in our culture, and most people don't even know it. In the pages ahead, you're going to meet young people just like you who have rediscovered this better way—a way to reach higher, dream bigger, grow stronger, love and honor God, live with more joy—and quit wasting their lives.

In *Do Hard Things,* we not only say there is a better way to do the teen years, we show you how we and thousands of other teens are doing it right now and how you can as well.

THE BIRTH OF A BIG IDEA

Rumblings of a rebelution

The summer of 2005, when we were sixteen, was a tough summer—not so much because of what we did but because of what we didn't do. For several years we had been heavily involved in high-school speech and debate, spending most of our summers doing research for the next season's topic and writing speeches for individual events. Our parents had decided that it was time for us to move on, and while we agreed with their decision, we felt lost.

We welcomed the break, but we were looking for direction—unsure of what to do with our lives, or even of what came next. We knew that we wanted to do something that mattered, but what was it? It seemed like every time we thought we had a plan, God closed the door. We were floating. In limbo.

Then Dad took charge.

"I'm putting you two on an intense reading program this summer," he announced one morning, placing a large stack of books on the kitchen counter.

We eyed one another warily. We love to read, but something about the way dad said the word *intense* caught our attention—that and the thickness of the books he was pointing to. The stack included books on a huge range of topics: history, philosophy, theology, sociology, science, business, journalism, and globalization.

For the next few months we didn't do much besides read. We digested books like *The Tipping Point* by Malcolm Gladwell, *The Rise of Theodore Roosevelt* by Edmund Morris, *Total Truth* by Nancy Pearcey, *The Fabric of the Cosmos* by Brian Greene, *Blog* by Hugh Hewitt, and *The World Is Flat* by Thomas Friedman, to name a few. The more we read, the more our minds were filled with exciting—and at the same time troubling—thoughts about our rapidly changing world and our generation's place in it.

We began to realize that even though the books we were reading were all written for adults, teens were the ones who most needed to wake up to what the books were saying. After all, aren't teens the ones who will grow up to live in the world those books describe? And aren't teens the ones who will be called on to lead it? If so, we were convinced that there had to be more to the teen years than pop culture suggests.

We decided to start a blog as a place to share our thoughts with friends and any others who might stumble across it. We knew we needed to let our ideas out, and the Internet was clearly the way to go. After some back-and-forth, we finally settled on a name for our blog: The Rebelution.

The word *rebelution* is probably new to you. To be honest, we made it up. We combined *rebellion* and *revolution* to form an entirely new word for an entirely new concept: rebelling against rebellion. More precisely, we define *rebelution* as "a teenage rebellion against low expectations."

In this chapter we want to show you the personal side of the Rebelution because that's how it started—as two teens waking up to a big idea, and the first rumblings of a historic shift in the thinking of teens across the country and around the world. This chapter is our story. In the chapters that follow, we lay out in more detail why we think the Rebelution is necessary, what it stands for, and how you can be part of it.

STRIKING THE RIGHT CHORD

If you had told us then that our humble Google-hosted blog sporting a generic design template would go on to become the most popular Christian teen blog on the web, we would've laughed. But our ideas about what God can do through teens like us have come a long way since then.

One of the first series of articles we posted was called *The Myth of Adolescence,* calling into question the modern notion of the teen years as a time to goof off. Almost immediately other teens started to comment on our posts. To our surprise we found that teens didn't just think that the teen years *could* have deeper meaning, they felt strongly that the teen years *should* have deeper meaning. "What you're saying is what I'm missing at my church," wrote one teen. "Don't stop!"

When we asked on the blog why teens weren't rising up against our culture's low expectations, the response overwhelmed us. "Everyone I know at school is shackled by low expectations," commented sixteen-year-old Lauren from Colorado. Nate, a high-school senior from Florida, wrote, "Man, did you ever say exactly what I've been feeling, well, ever since I became a teenager!"

As the conversation heated up, we kept wondering who exactly these other teens were. Some of them we knew, but most of them we didn't. Were they all overachieving, Type A, head-of-their-class types? When we asked, we discovered that wasn't the case. Most described themselves as normal, every-day teens. Some were public schooled, some private, some homeschooled. Most lived in the United States; others wrote from Canada, the United Kingdom, Australia, Brazil, and the Philippines. How they found us we don't really know. But most of them were restless. Our questions had struck a chord.

Word spread. New questions sparked more discussion and inspired new blog posts—sometimes two or more a day. We didn't have all the answers, and not many who wrote in thought they did either. But all the asking and arguing, push-ing and probing, helped sharpen our rough ideas. Something big was starting to unfold.

A lot bigger than we realized. Just three weeks after the blog was launched, the *New York Daily News,* the sixth-largest daily newspaper in the United States, wrote a feature column about the blog. "Think Big! HS Twins Tell Peers" read the headline. The column opened with the words, "Most high schoolers' blogs are the online equivalent of perfumed diaries or locker-room walls—outlets for teens to gossip, confess and network with their pals. But a pair of 16-year-old home-schooled twins from Oregon...are out to change that."

"The teen years are not a vacation from responsibility," we had told the columnist. "They are the training ground of future leaders who dare to be responsible now."

The article drew more readers to the blog. Most were just curious that a group of teens was actually *looking* for responsibility, but a lot of people stuck around, and the heavy traffic didn't interrupt the real discussion that was going on among the growing ranks of "rebelutionaries."

"Assume we teens get this," wrote Jake, a junior from Oklahoma, responding to a new post on low expectations in media. "What do we really need to do? What's next?"

God must have been following our online discussion—and smiling. Because what He brought us next blew our old expectations for the teen years into tiny pieces.

GUINEA PIGS FOR OUR OWN IDEAS

In October 2005, we were invited to apply for an internship at the Alabama Supreme Court. Say that again? Never in a million years could we have predicted anything like that. Those positions were generally reserved for law school students and exceptional college undergraduates. We'd been successful in speech and debate competition, yes, but we hadn't even graduated from high school. We were still sixteen years old.

Our first thought was that they must not have known how old we were. But they did. It turned out that the staff attorney in charge of the intern program in Justice Tom Parker's office had been reading The Rebelution blog and decided he was willing to take us up on our premise that teens have—and waste—enormous untapped potential. At the staff attorney's request, Justice Parker agreed to waive the usual age requirement for interns and look solely at whether we could do the job. The door was open. The ball was in our court.

We chose to apply for the internship, but honestly, we didn't know what to fear more—getting rejected or getting accepted. An agonizing month went by. Finally word came. We had been accepted for a two-month internship in the chambers of a supreme court justice. Our primary responsibilities would be to research and proof judicial opinions for Justice Parker. Our start date would fall two weeks before we turned seventeen.

As excited as we were to be accepted, we also felt enormous pressure. We would be the youngest interns in the history of the Alabama Supreme Court—possibly of any supreme court. It's not that we didn't bring some skills to the table. We had worked hard to become proficient researchers, debaters, and writers. But that was junior high and high school. This was a whole new level. God seemed to be making us the guinea pigs for our own ideas. Only fair, we see now, but at the time we were terrified.

We were leaving home for the first time, and we had less than a month to get ready. We would be wearing a suit and tie every day, which meant several hectic shopping trips downtown. We also had to make living arrangements, and of course we had to let our blog readers know what was going on.

They were excited. Everybody understood that this was a chance for the two of us to try out the ideas our web community had been discussing so intently. It was time to live the message of our little movement—not just read and write about it.

Upon our arrival in Montgomery, we learned that we'd be expected to contribute in a variety of ways, and training would be entirely on-the-job. Though Justice Parker and his staff were gracious and inclusive, we wouldn't be receiving any special treatment. They had ignored our age when they considered us for the internship, and they would ignore it now when it came to evaluating our performance. We would have to earn trust, and we would not be allowed to compromise the efficiency of the court.

This meant that we started with the basics—picking up the mail, making photocopies, and organizing papers. We also drafted press releases and handled certain e-mail correspondence. Soon we were invited to help edit Justice Parker's opinions and circulate them to other justices. Every time one job went well, Justice Parker trusted us with more. In fact, his expectation that we could do more was a constant motivation to learn and improve.

By the end of two months, we had gone from running errands to accompanying Justice Parker to prestigious events.

We had gone from editing opinions for punctuation and spelling to actually contributing paragraphs of final wording, even occasionally drafting internal memorandums to the other justices. By the time our internship was up, even Justice Parker was surprised by what we had accomplished—and we were elated.

Right away another door opened: we were invited back to Alabama to serve as grass-roots directors for four simultaneous statewide campaigns for the Alabama Supreme Court—including Justice Parker's run for chief justice.

The guinea pigs had survived! More important, both of us had experienced our own personal rebelution. And that was just the beginning.

RACING ACROSS THE STATE

Our internships tested two young men, but the statewide campaigns would test a whole team of teens. Hundreds of them, in fact. As grass-roots directors we'd be working with and recruiting young people and their families to head up efforts around the state. And we would operate under the same guideline that had gotten us the job: ability, not age, would determine who was recruited.

The spring of 2006 found us back in Alabama, ready to take the Rebelution movement to the next level. We were stationed at campaign headquarters in Montgomery, but over the next three months we visited almost every county in the state. All of the core members of the campaign staff were on the younger side. Our campaign manager was by far the oldest, in his midthirties; our field director was twenty-three; and we, the grass-roots directors, were seventeen. That was just the start. One of the first people we recruited was Jake Smith—the same Jake who had written in with the question "What do we really need to do? What's next?"

We recruited teenagers at almost every level of the campaign and encouraged them to take on high-level responsibility. Teens designed the campaign website. Teens coordinated housing and meals for out-of-state volunteers. Teens used advanced mapping software to create driving routes for literature drops. They planned events and coordinated television coverage. They provided graphic design, campaign photography, and videography. By the time the campaign was over, teens had not only worked thousands of hours on the campaign, but had also put together the largest grass-roots operation in any Alabama race that season.

But with big dreams come big challenges. You wouldn't believe some of the problems we had to solve, usually with no warning. For example:

- How do you recruit and remotivate volunteers who had showed up only because they were mistakenly told they'd be working for a *different* candidate?

- How do you distribute 120,000 newspapers at a NASCAR race at Talladega Superspeedway in thirty-six hours (without getting run over or arrested)?
- Where do you house volunteers who drive in from four states away and arrive tired, broke, and *way too early*?
- What do you say to older recruits—mostly college kids, as it turned out—who loudly proclaim that teenagers are clueless punks and not to be trusted, and then find out that *you* (that is, "clueless punks") are the ones in charge?

But with every challenge, our entire team discovered new opportunities to learn, laugh, and sometimes start over. We also made discoveries about ourselves as individuals. A campaign—like any movement or revolution—isn't really a faceless mass. It's a collection of individuals who join together on the same cause for a reason. It's ordinary people who decide to step out and be part of something big.

That's when they become extraordinary.

Shy Girl in Charge

We wish you could meet Heidi Bentley, our coordinator for Mobile County. We had met Heidi and her family briefly at the campaign kickoff meeting. In the following weeks, all our communications with her were by phone or e-mail—she was in southern Alabama and we were in the capitol. We gave

Heidi all sorts of big assignments—everything from handing out campaign materials at large festivals to booking facilities and making hundreds of phone calls—and she did an incredible job. We'd often say to one another, "If all of our county coordinators were like Heidi, we'd be in great shape!"

But Heidi was not who we thought she was. We had gotten her mixed up with her older sister, whom we'd also met at the kickoff. The whole time we thought Heidi was twenty-four. The real Heidi was seventeen.

Our first reaction was, *Oh man, I can't believe we asked so much of her!* Then we caught ourselves. Wait a second! We thought she was twenty-four, so we had expected her to be responsible as if she were twenty-four, and she rose to meet those expectations and acted like she was twenty-four. Heidi was a one-person testimonial for the Rebelution we'd been blogging about.

Our second reaction was, *Duh! We're seventeen too, and we're the grass-roots directors, for crying out loud!*

But it was only toward the end of the campaign that we learned something else about Heidi. She had always been extremely introverted. She hated talking on the phone, her family told us, even with people she knew. Yet we had put her on the phone with strangers almost constantly. Throughout the entire campaign, her family watched in amazement as Heidi jumped way outside of her comfort zone and did things that would have seemed impossible before.

BETTER THAN SUCCESS

When we tell the story of the Alabama campaigns, people always ask whether we won. The answer is no. Despite the competence and hard work of so many people like Heidi, our candidates lost at the polls. Ironically, the very day we sat down to write this story, the *Huntsville Times* published an editorial titled "Judicial-Race Excesses." It chided the campaigns for their "out-of-control" spending. The 2006 Alabama judicial races, the paper reported, had set the all-time national high of fifteen million dollars. Out of that amount, our four candidates combined spent less than half a million dollars. We like to think that the unprecedented level of teenage involvement had something to do with the unprecedented level of spending it took to beat us!

Shortly after the campaigns ended, Heidi wrote to us to share what she felt God had been doing in her life:

During this whole campaign, God has been doing amazing things. I think I have grown more in these past few months than the whole year before!

I laughed when I first read the phrase "do hard things." That's exactly what God began to teach me with the beginning of the campaign, and it hasn't stopped with primaries. He has taken my perspective

of my own capabilities and stretched it three times
around a new and bigger perspective.

I think I have thoroughly shocked my family
by doing things that they (and I) never imagined
I'd be doing. It's amazing what we can do if we will
trust God enough to step out of our comfort zones!

We look back with gratitude, realizing that we gained so
much: learning to trust God, for example, or finding that
stepping outside of our comfort zones helped us grow, or realizing that together young people can accomplish much more
than our culture gives us credit for. Working on the campaigns taught us that never trying is a lot worse than losing.
And we experienced firsthand that all effort—even failed
effort—produces muscle. In fact, because of our work in
Alabama, the agenda for the Rebelution that we'd been talking about back home snapped into sharper focus—particularly what we began to call the three pillars of the Rebelution:
character, competence, and collaboration (but more about
them later).

The first two stages of our personal rebelution—the internship and the campaigns—had moved us from the personal
experience of two teens to the community experience of
many.

The next stage launched us into the virtual experience of
millions.

REBELUTION RISING

When we arrived home from Alabama, we were excited about refocusing on the online community that had continued to form. Quickly we decided that we needed to take the blog to the next level—launching a full website that would offer additional resources and ways for rebelutionaries to interact with one another.

Actually, we'd never planned to have a full-blown website of our own. But the community was already there, so it seemed only natural that the website follow. We hired a friend to do the coding for us while we designed everything and figured out where it should go. To go along with a completely new look and feel, the website would feature discussion forums, links to hundreds of other articles by great authors (past and present), and a conference section outlining our plan to hold four regional events during 2007. Weeks of planning and several all-nighters later, the website launched on August 28, 2006—the one-year anniversary of The Rebelution blog.

It was our first time creating a website, but we were able to pull in other guys from around the country (and even outside the country) to help us get the project done on time. Alex King, a sixteen-year-old from Maine; Alex Poythress, a seventeen-year-old from Alabama; and David Boskovic, a seventeen-year-old from Canada, stayed up late and got up early to put the finishing touches on the website so it could be launched at 6:00 a.m.

Then we waited to see what would happen.

The response was instantaneous and overwhelming. Despite the fact that we did next to nothing to promote the launch, our traffic jumped from around 2,200 hits the previous day to 12,800 hits on launch day—a 480 percent increase in traffic overnight. It wasn't a generic-looking blog anymore. It was an entire online community.

REBELLING AGAINST REBELLION

It's been over two years since our dad dropped that big stack of books on the kitchen counter and brought our aimless summer to a screeching halt. Since then, our website has received over fifteen million hits from several million unique visitors around the world. We've hosted Rebelution conferences across the United States—and internationally, in Japan. At our last 2007 conference in Indianapolis, over twenty-one hundred people showed up—some driving as many as sixteen hours to be there.

What God has done since the summer of 2005 has been incredible. We're just blessed to be along for the ride. Sure, we came up with a name for it, but the Rebelution is something God is doing in the hearts of our generation, not something we engineered. That's why the purpose of this book is not to brag about anything we've done, but to talk about something huge that God is doing in the lives of young people around the world—something He wants to do in your life as well.

If you look back over history, you'll find other movements that were started (or fueled) by young people. The problem is, most of these movements were actually revolts against God-established authority (like parents, church, or government), and many were ultimately crushed or twisted toward another end.

All those failed revolutionary attempts are a discouraging record as far as teen efforts go, but not for rebelutionaries. We're not rebelling against institutions or even against people. Our uprising is against a cultural mind-set that twists the purpose and potential of the teen years and threatens to cripple our generation. Our uprising won't be marked by mass riots and violence, but by millions of individual teens quietly choosing to turn the low expectations of our culture upside down.

That is our invitation to you—to join with us and other teenagers who are serious about changing the world's ideas about the teen years.

In the upcoming chapters, we'll show you how.

THE MYTH OF ADOLESCENCE

Exposing the low expectations that are robbing our generation

D o you know anyone who owns an elephant? Neither do we. We grew up with all the usual pets. Some unusual ones too—rats, snakes, wild ducklings, turtles, salamanders, a great horned owl, even a baby white-tailed deer.

But we never had an elephant.

That didn't stop us from dreaming. We could just picture it: Some kid would brag, "Hey, our family just got a dog! A purebred schnauzerdoodle-something! He fetches and sits and everything!"

"That's great," we'd reply. "Our family just got an elephant."

From that moment on, we'd be twin rulers of the playground. "Hey, bring your purebred schnauzerdoodle over sometime. Bet our pet can sit on your pet."

Or something like that.

When we got older, we learned a bit more about elephants. For example, in certain parts of Asia, farmers still use elephants to do much of their heavy labor. Elephants pull stumps and trees out of the ground, haul logs, and carry heavy loads. They're good at it too, because not only are they enormous, they're also incredibly strong.

Some countries hold "elephant festivals" to celebrate the strength, agility, and intelligence of these mighty animals. Handlers enter the elephants in games of basketball and soccer—with giant balls. Elephants perform choreographed dances to music. But the main event is a game of tug of war between an elephant and one hundred grown men.

Let's think about this for a moment. We're half-Japanese, so let's say the average Asian man in this tug-of-war competition is our size—about 135 pounds. Not too impressive (we're working on that). Still, when you multiply that by one hundred, that's six whole tons. Plus, the men aren't just standing around. They're digging in their heels and *pulling*.

But the elephant still wins—every time.

That information made us question our childhood dream of owning an elephant. For example, what would we do if our elephant woke up in the middle of the night and decided it wanted to visit Aunt Bertha and Uncle Dumbo?

Later we learned that elephant owners in Asia don't have this problem. To keep their elephants from wandering off, they have a surprisingly simple solution. The owner takes a small rope, ties it to a wooden post in the ground, and attaches it to the elephant's right hind leg. That's it.

Of course, to the elephant the rope is nothing more than string. One jerk and the rope would snap. One kick and the post would go flying. Yet with nothing but the small rope holding it back, the elephant stays put. It won't move from the spot.

How is that possible? The answer is that it has little to do with the piece of rope around the elephant's ankle and everything to do with the invisible shackles around the elephant's mind.

Over the past few years, instead of wishing to own an elephant, we began to suspect that we might *be* elephants.

Could it be that we and most young people we know are like that elephant—strong, smart, holding incredible potential, but somehow held back by nothing more than a piece of twine? Left almost powerless by a lie?

We think so. And we've come to believe that a big part of what holds us back as a generation is a harmless-sounding but very powerful idea we call the Myth of Adolescence.

BEFORE THERE WAS MYSPACE

The word *teenager* is so common today that most people don't even think about it—and if they do, it's usually not positive. According to the dictionary, a teenager is a person between the ages of thirteen and nineteen years old. There's a good chance you fall in that category. Like most teens, you attend school, have a MySpace or Facebook profile, and are more likely to take a photo with your phone than with a camera.

But would it surprise you to find out that at one time teenagers didn't even exist? Don't believe us? How about a pop quiz?

The first documented use of the word *teenager* was:

(a) Tyndale's first edition English *New Testament* in 1526.

(b) Shakespeare's *Romeo and Juliet* in 1623.

(c) Benjamin Franklin's *Poor Richard's Almanac* in 1739.

(d) Theodore Roosevelt's *Strenuous Life* speech in 1899.

(e) A *Reader's Digest* issue in 1941.

(f) Alex and Brett made it up for this book.

The answer is (e). That's right, the word *teenager* has been around for less than seventy years.

Prior to the early twentieth century and, really, throughout history, people were either children or adults. Family and work were the primary occupations of the group we now call teenagers. In fact, in 1900 only one out of ten American young people between fourteen and seventeen years old attended high school. One historian, Friedrich Heer, writes about that era, focusing on Europe:

> Around 1,800 young people of both sexes could reckon
> on being considered adults as soon as the outward
> signs of puberty made their appearance. Girls attained
> marriageable age at fifteen.... Boys could join the
> Prussian army as officer cadets at the age of fifteen.
> Among the upper classes entry to university or to a
> profession was possible at the age of fifteen or sixteen.
> The school leaving age, and consequently the end of
> childhood, was *raised* during the nineteenth century
> to fourteen.

So what was it like to be a teen back then, before the idea of teens even existed? Good question. To answer it, we'd like to introduce you to three young people from different times in America's past. Their names are George, David, and Clara.

GEORGE, DAVID, AND CLARA

George was born in northern Virginia in 1732 to a middle-class family. When he was eleven years old, he lost his father. Even though his peers never considered him very bright, he applied himself to his studies and mastered geometry, trigonometry, and surveying (think algebra and calculus) by the time he was sixteen.

At seventeen years old, George had the chance to put his studies to use at his first job. Talk about a job! Official surveyor of Culpeper County, Virginia. This wasn't a boy's job, and it certainly wasn't office work. For the next three years George endured the hardships of frontier life as he measured and recorded previously unmapped territories. His measuring tools were heavy logs and chains. George was a man at seventeen.

David was born in 1801 near the city of Knoxville, Tennessee, where his father was serving in the state militia. At ten years old, David began a career at sea, serving as a naval cadet on the warship *Essex*. At eleven he saw his first battle.

At age twelve, David was given command of a ship that had been captured in battle and was dispatched with a crew to take the vessel and its men back to the United States. On the journey home, the captured British captain took issue at being ordered around by a twelve-year-old and announced that he was going below to get his pistols (out of respect for his position, he had been allowed to keep them). David promptly sent him word that if he stepped foot on deck with his pistols, he would be shot and thrown overboard. The captain decided to stay below.

Clara was born in Oxford, Massachusetts, on Christmas Day, 1821. She was the baby of the family, with ten years separating her and the next youngest. She was a timid child, so terrified of strangers that she was hardly able to speak. Then something happened that would change her life forever. When she was eleven years old, her older brother David fell from the roof of a barn and was seriously injured. Young Clara was frantic and begged to help care for him.

Once in the sickroom, Clara surprised everyone by demonstrating all the qualities of an experienced nurse. She learned better than anyone how to make her brother comfortable. Little by little, the doctor allowed her to take over all of his care, with his complete recovery lasting two years.

A year later, at the age of fourteen, Clara became the nurse for her father's hired man, who had come down with smallpox, and then to more patients as the epidemic spread through the Massachusetts village where she lived. Still shy and timid, her desire to serve others drove her to overcome her fears. By age seventeen she was a successful schoolteacher with over forty students—some nearly as old as she.

All three of these young people were given increasing levels of responsibility at early ages, and they not only survived, they rose to the occasion. Even more important, as the quote we shared from Professor Heer shows, *at the time in which they lived, young men and women like them were not all that unusual.*

The question is: what changed? Why is it that young men and women of the past were able to do things (and do them well) at fifteen or sixteen that many of today's twenty-five to thirty-year-olds can't do?

Is it because young people are now called "teenagers"? Not exactly.

The answer is that people today view the teen years through the modern lens of adolescence—a social category of age and behavior that would have been completely foreign to men and women not too long ago.

The term *adolescence* literally means "to grow up." This is true in a biological sense as well as in other aspects of maturity. We have no problem with that, or even with the word itself— you'll notice that we still use the word *teenager* a lot. The problem we have is with the modern understanding of adolescence that allows, encourages, and even trains young people to remain childish for much longer than necessary. It holds us back from what we *could* do, from what God *made* us to do, and even from what we would *want* to do if we got out from under society's low expectations.

For the powerful elephant, a shackle looks like a piece of twine. For young people today—a powerful, educated, and unusually blessed generation—our shackles hide in simple, deadly ideas like "adolescence" and "teenager."

Are you ready to set yourself free by changing how you think?

THE HISTORY OF YOU (STARTING ONE HUNDRED YEARS AGO)

In order to understand the modern "teenager" concept, we have to go back in time only a hundred years. At that time, right around the year 1900, a cascade of labor- and school-reform laws were passed in an attempt to protect kids from the harsh conditions in factories. These laws were good because conditions had been brutal, and children's health and education suffered. Unfortunately, the laws had some unintended and far-reaching consequences. By completely removing children from the workplace and mandating school attendance through high school, teens' once-established role as key producers and contributors came to an end. Suddenly their role was almost exclusively that of consumers.

Young people were suddenly stuck in a poorly defined category between childhood and adulthood. Young men and women like George, David, and Clara were discouraged. Instead, the "teenager" was invented—a young person with most of the desires and abilities of an adult but few of the expectations or responsibilities.

When we were researching this subject, we happened across a word origins book called *America in So Many Words*. Read what it says about the word *teenager*.

In the first part of the twentieth century, we made a startling discovery. There were teenagers among us! Until then, we had thought of people in just two stages: children and adults. And while childhood might have its tender moments, the goal of the child was to grow up as promptly as possible in order to enjoy the opportunities and shoulder the responsibilities of an adult. The girl became the woman, the boy became the man. It was as simple and significant as that....

[But] [t]he reforms of the early twentieth century, preventing child labor and mandating education through high school, lengthened the pre-adult years. In earlier times, a person reaching adult size at age thirteen or fourteen was ready to do adult work. Now adult size was achieved as soon as ever, but preparation for adult responsibilities lasted until age eighteen or later.

Thus the years ending in -*teen* became something new and distinctive.... The teenager remade our world. The concept is...subversive: why should any teenager enjoying freedom submit to the authority of adults?

With the discovery of this new age, ours has been the century of the teenager ever since.

Think about that last line: "Ours has been the century of the teenager ever since." Isn't that exactly what has happened? Entire industries—movie, music, fashion, fast food—and countless online services revolve around the consumer habits of, you guessed it, teens.

With all this money and attention focused on teens, the teen years are viewed as some sort of vacation. Society doesn't expect much of anything from young people during their teen years—except trouble. And it certainly doesn't expect competence, maturity, or productivity. The saddest part is that, as the culture around them has come to expect less and less, young people have dropped to meet those lower expectations. Since most of us have grown up surrounded by these low expectations, meeting them is like breathing to us—we never give it a thought. And we never realize what we've lost.

As one education expert put it, "Our current ceiling for students is really much closer to where the floor ought to be." Think about that. The most our society expects from teens is really much closer to the least we should expect. Does that strike you as extreme? To us it seems extremely true. And not just in school but in every area of our lives.

So just how far have the expectations fallen?

MAKING OUR BEDS (AND OTHER FEATS OF VALOR)

Recently, we decided to Google the words *teens* and *expectations* to see what came up. The results were far more entertaining than we would have imagined.

Most web browsers have a built-in Google search box, and as you type in your search terms, it gives you suggested searches based on terms that are used most often. Here are some of the suggestions it gave us as we tried to Google *teens* and *expectations:*

- *teens and drugs*
- *teens and alcohol*
- *teens and smoking*
- *teens and drinking*
- *teens and marijuana*
- *teens and cell phones*

Even Google has low expectations for teens! Anyway, we did our search.

The top result was about teens, drugs, and alcohol abuse. Another was for an article called "A Parent's Guide to Surviving the Teen Years." But the one that really jumped out at us was an article about teaching teens responsibility by setting expectations.

The article seemed promising, so we clicked the link: "When you formally develop a set of expectations for your teen, you begin to set your teen up for succeeding in meeting those expectations." And so we're thinking, *This is great!*

But maybe not.

The author proceeded to list suggested expectations for teens, divided up by age group. First, preteens and younger teens, ages ten to fourteen. You are expected to...

- make your bed every day
- be able to take a message on the phone
- clean your room every week (with help from Mom and Dad)

Then comes older teens, fifteen and up. Besides everything on the younger teens' list, you are expected to...

- do a daily chore [just one], like taking out the trash
- make sure the gas gauge stays above a quarter of a tank
- clean your room every week (with no help from Mom and Dad)

The article also includes an encouragement to parents about the list: "Please do not feel that your teenager should be doing all of them." *Phew.* We were getting worried there!

The author means well. And actually for some teens, meeting those low expectations might require a great deal of effort. But consider for a minute how far the expectations have fallen. Seventeen-year-old George was expected to endure the hardships of frontier life as a surveyor. And we're expected to endure the hardships of doing the dinner dishes?

Twelve-year-old David was expected to successfully return a ship, its captain, and its crew to the United States. We are expected to return our pillows, sheets, and blankets to their proper place on the bed. David succeeded. Did you this morning?

It's almost gotten to the point that people expect less of teenagers than they do of toddlers. Think about it. Why do babies, with inferior motor skills, reasoning ability, and physical strength, experience nearly 100 percent success in overcoming difficult challenges, while teens often falter? Well, one is expected, and the other is not.

Why does every healthy baby learn to walk while very few teenagers have learned to dance? One is expected, and the other is not.

Why does every healthy baby overcome communication barriers by learning to talk while very few teenagers overcome barriers between themselves and their parents by learning to communicate? One is expected, and the other is not.

The truth is that all of us are susceptible to low expectations. Once we have satisfied the minimum requirements, we tend to stop pushing ourselves.

The Surprising Power of Expectations

You're probably familiar with the saying "Ideas have consequences." But did you know that expectations have consequences? It's true. The power of expectations has been documented in study after study over the last few decades. We're familiar with two of them—one occurring in a public middle school in San Francisco, the other at a Bible college in our hometown of Portland, Oregon.

Both studies were set up the same way. Teachers were given two classes of randomly divided students. However, the teachers were told that one class was made up of the best and brightest students at the school and that the other class was made up of the slower to average students. With that, the teachers began to teach. And guess what happened?

All of the teachers' interactions with the students were tainted by their expectations. When the teachers worked with a student in the "bright" class, they persisted with the student until he or she found the answer. But when a student in the "slow" class didn't find the answer right away, the teachers moved on to another student. When a student in the bright class struggled, the teachers brushed it off, saying that the student was just having an "off day." But when the students in the slow class struggled, it was just because they were slow.

Don't miss this: statistically the classes were exactly the same. The only difference was in what their teachers *expected* of them. Soon, the students began to meet those expectations. The "best and brightest" class began to excel, and the "slower to average" class began to lag behind.

As teens, we're no different from the middle school and

college students in those studies. For all of us, expectations are a self-fulfilling prophecy. In the words of Henry Ford, founder of the Ford Motor Company, "Whether you think you can or whether you think you can't, you're right."

The self-fulfilling power of expectations impacts teens in almost every area—often maddeningly so. Take, for example, tech savvy and sexual activity. These are two areas where teens are expected to have high interest and high performance. Just as you'd predict, the levels of activity, consumption, and even obsession in these areas are unprecedented. We are meeting the expectations set before us.

Isn't it ironic that many teenagers, though fluent in multiple computer languages (we're considered trendsetters and early adopters), are not expected to understand or care about things like personal finances, politics, or our faith? We're not even expected to be capable of carrying on an intelligent conversation with an adult.

Isn't something wrong when girls are constantly judged on their physical appearance and pressed to become more and more sexually provocative, yet are so rarely expected to develop qualities of character and intellect beneath the surface?

When we understand the power of expectations, we begin to understand why things have changed so dramatically and why our culture has bought into the Myth of Adolescence—without even realizing that it doesn't have to be true.

What the Bible Says About Teens

You might wonder what the Bible has to say about adolescence. The answer is simple.

Nothing.

You won't find the words *teenager* or *adolescence* anywhere in Scripture. And you won't find any reference to a period of time between childhood and adulthood either. Instead you'll find the apostle Paul writing in 1 Corinthians 13:11, "When I was a child, I spoke like a child, I thought like a child, I reasoned like a child. When I became a man, I gave up childish ways."

Notice what he didn't say. He didn't say, "When I was a child, I spoke like a child, I thought like a child, I reasoned like a child. But then I became a teenager and I looked like an adult, I sounded like an adult, but I still acted like a child." No! He said, "I became a man, and I gave up childish ways."

In another letter, Paul wrote to a young pastor in training: "Don't let anyone look down on you because you are young, but set an example for the believers in speech, in life, in love, in faith and in purity" (1 Timothy 4:12, NIV).

What we find here is clear evidence that God does not hold two standards: one for young adults and one for adults. He has high expectations for both. Where some might look down on or excuse young adults, God calls us to be examples. Where our culture might expect little, God expects great things.

So whose expectations are we living by? The Bible says, "Do not conform any longer to the pattern of this world" (Romans 12:2, NIV). When we let cultural expectations become our standard, we allow ourselves to be squeezed into a mold, with little room for Christlike character or competence.

As we have seen in this chapter—and as you no doubt know from personal experience—we live in a culture that wants to tell us how to act, how to think, how to look, and how to talk. It tells us what to wear, what to buy, and where to buy it. It tells us what to dream, what to value, what to live for—and it's not Christ. To quote an old Pepsi ad from the nineties, "Be young. Have fun. Drink Pepsi." Nike tells us, "Just do it." Sprite tells us, "Obey your thirst." And who hasn't heard the joke that 92 percent of teens would be dead if trend-setting Hollister decided breathing was uncool?

Where expectations are high, we tend to rise to meet them. Where expectations are low, we tend to drop to meet them. And yet this is the exact opposite of what we're told to do in 1 Corinthians 14:20: "Brothers, stop thinking like children. In regard to evil be infants, but in your thinking be adults" (NIV). Our culture says, "Be mature in evil, but in your thinking and behavior be childish."

Of course, sometimes we *like* being able to do things we know we shouldn't do—or getting away with less than our best. We excuse our choices because that's what teens are *supposed* to do or by thinking, *Well, I'm not as bad as some people*

I know. We go with the crowd. We do what comes easily: we certainly don't do hard things.

The consequence? We waste some of the best years of our lives and never reach our full God-given potential. We never attempt things that would stretch, grow, and strengthen us. We end up weak and unprepared for the amazing future that could have been. We like the freedom low expectations give us, but we're really being robbed.

As the stories in this book will show you, wasting our teen years is not what most of us *really* want. And it's not what God wants for us either.

BREAKING THE TWINE

Remember our elephant in India, shackled by nothing but a piece of twine and a wooden post in the ground? What's going on there? Why doesn't he just break free? The strength is there. Why doesn't he use it?

Here's how it works. When the elephant is still young, his owner takes him from his mother and shackles him to a large tree—with a heavy chain around his right hind leg. For days and weeks, the young elephant will strain and pull, trying to break free, but all he succeeds in doing is causing the shackle to cut deep into his leg. Eventually he gives up and accepts the idea that he can't go anywhere when there is something around his right hind leg.

Soon the owner can replace the tree with a post and the chain with a piece of twine. Once the elephant feels resistance, he stops. There's nothing but a piece of twine around his ankle, but there are heavy shackles around his mind.

In this book we hope to demonstrate that we—Alex and Brett, you, teenagers everywhere—are like that elephant. We have proven strength and God-given potential—the potential to do hard, important things—but we are held captive by a lie. We have been conditioned to believe what is false, to stop when things feel hard, and to miss out on God's incredible purpose for our teen years.

In the chapters that follow, we want to show you that deep down you want to do hard things, that you were created to do hard things, and what's more, you *can* do hard things. What you'll discover is a whole new way of living your teen years and of living the rest of your life. God's Word and all of history demonstrate that we are far more capable than we think. This world is trying to trap you by tying its pathetic piece of twine around your ankle. We want to help you break the twine.

This is what we call the Rebelution: throwing off the shackles of lies and low expectations and returning our generation to a true and very exciting understanding of the teen years—not as a vacation from responsibility but as a launching pad for the rest of our lives.

What does that look like? We'll find out in chapter 4.

A BETTER WAY

Reclaiming the teen years as the launching pad of life

Raymond is eighteen years old and lives in Baltimore, Maryland. His parents divorced when he was fourteen, and Raymond is involved in everything you can think of: smoking, drinking, drugs—even drug dealing. He moves from house to house, crashing with various friends, and has struggled to hold even the most basic jobs.

When he looks at the direction his life has taken, he

expresses regret. "When I first went to high school, my understanding was like, 'Wow, this is the time to party. It's high school, everybody's supposed to party in high school.' I don't know," he says. "I wish I wouldn't have thought that."

Raymond insists that he's not going to do drugs forever. He plans to sober up, get his GED, and move on with life. Someday he hopes to own a car dealership and sell BMWs. To help keep his dream alive, he subscribes to *duPont Registry,* a magazine about luxury cars, houses, and boats. When he's older, he plans to go to church more too.

"I think about my future a few times a week," he says. "What do I want to do with my life? Do I want to sit around and be a pothead all my life?" No, he says.

And so why not change now?

"I don't know," Raymond replies. "I've thought about it, but I kinda look at this as the summer to have fun and party, 'cause I'm eighteen years old, and I don't have to worry about living under my mom's roof, [so] I can be out as long as I want. So I'm like, 'This will be a summer for fun; I'm gonna party and have fun this summer.' Then after that I just want to sober up and be clean and get my life together and straighten up.

"But I don't want the future to get here too quick," he adds. "I want to be able to live life and still have fun."

There's probably a little bit of Raymond in all of us. Do you see him in you or in people you know? His views reflect the thinking of so many in our generation. Like many teens, he figures that he has plenty of time. At any point in the future, he can decide to clean up, grow up, and pick up his life as if nothing happened.

But is he right about that?

Is it really as simple as flipping a switch, or is Raymond in for a rude awakening? Will he go down as one of those guys who *thought* he was getting what he wanted out of life, only to realize he was actually wasting his teen years and putting his future at risk?

In this chapter we'll take a quick look at a whole group of people like Raymond. In fact, we'll even give them a name. Then we'll show you the huge opportunities they're missing out on. But just to warn you: we're going to use words Raymond probably wouldn't like. Because we describe these huge opportunities as five kinds of *hard things* that have the power to launch us from where we are now to our best possible future.

But first, what do we mean when we talk about being launched?

FAILURE TO LAUNCH

We took swimming lessons when we were kids, but growing up in the rainy Pacific Northwest, we didn't really swim a whole lot. In other words, don't expect us to demonstrate any nifty strokes or perform crazy flips off the high dive. It's not happening.

One thing we did learn, though, was that diving boards have a "sweet spot." If you take a big leap and land on it just right, the diving board will launch you up into the air and down into the pool in a perfect swan dive. You hope. Of course, if you miss the sweet spot, things don't work out so well. Your body jolts, the board clunks, and you bounce, teeter, and career into the water. You may even do a belly flop. In fact, if someone's watching, you're *guaranteed* to do a belly flop.

But back to the big picture. Do you see it?

The pool is your future life. The diving board is your present life. The Myth of Adolescence would have you think that now is your time to party beside the pool. But the fact is, you're already on the diving board.

The whole purpose of the diving board is to launch us, with purpose and precision, into our futures. We will either make a successful dive into adulthood or deliver something closer to a belly flop—a failure to launch.

In his book *Thoughts for Young Men,* J. C. Ryle wrote, "Youth is the seed-time of full age, the molding season in the little space of human life, the turning-point in the history of man's mind." In other words, what each of us will become later in life largely depends on what we become now. Are we taking that seriously?

In 1 Corinthians 9:24–25, the apostle Paul writes, "Run in such a way as to get the prize. Everyone who competes in the games goes into *strict training.* They do it to get a crown that will not last; but we do it to get a crown that will last forever" (NIV).

We are convinced that the teen years are the primary time God has given to us for "strict training." We can hear Raymond saying, "Strict training! You've *got* to be kidding!" But stick with us.

Proverbs 20:29 says, "The glory of young men is their strength." Did you catch that? At no other time are we better positioned to decide who we will become. Our strength—sharp minds, energetic bodies, and flexible schedules—is our glory. We are not likely to have this same set of strengths ever again. By choosing to use our teen years for strict training, we can choose to set direction, develop character, and build momentum for an amazing future.

But what happens when we fail to use our teen years for strict training? What does a belly flop in real life look like? Unfortunately, it's not too difficult to find out.

THE RISE OF THE KIDULT

In 2005, *Time* magazine ran a story on "kidults," a new breed of adolescents in their mid- to late twenties and beyond who offer convincing evidence that the modern concept of adolescence is not a biological stage, but a cultural mind-set. It doesn't stop when you graduate from high school, or when you turn twenty-one.

"Everybody knows a few of them," the article pronounced. "Full-grown men and women who still live with their parents, who dress and talk and party as they did in their teens, hopping from job to job and date to date, having fun but seemingly going nowhere."

Kidults generally have neither clear direction nor a sense of urgency. "Legally, they're adults, but they're on the threshold, the doorway to adulthood, and they're not going through it," says Terri Apter, a psychologist at the University of Cambridge. In other words, they're standing on the end of the diving board, but they won't jump in.

And it's not just in America. Countries around the world have developed names for young "adults" like this: they're called "kippers" in England, "nesthockers" in Germany, "mammones" in France, and "freeters" in Japan.

"This isn't just a trend, a temporary fad or a generational hiccup," the article warns. "This is a much larger phenomenon, of a different kind and a different order."

But we shouldn't be surprised. After all, kidults are the logical result of the Myth of Adolescence, which encourages teens to view adulthood as spoiling the fun of the teen years rather than viewing it as the fulfillment of the teen years.

Being taught to avoid growing up doesn't help us launch into adulthood. At best, it leaves us hanging on the end of the diving board—stuck in the childishness and irresponsibility of adolescence. At worst, it leaves us floundering in the deep end of the pool—unprepared for the exciting challenges of life.

We received this e-mail in July of 2007, but it represents many conversations we've had with people in their twenties, even early thirties:

> I had my own idea of fun, which was too much recreational reading, too much playing video games, too much of my own thing. To this day, I've never held a job, and I'm still living at home. My lack of real life skills has had some very negative consequences to a relationship that is very important to me.
>
> When I was a teenager, twenty-six seemed so far away, but my bad decisions then (to do nothing) are affecting my life now in some pretty serious ways.
>
> I'm an example of how low expectations and our "if it's fun, do it" culture can mess things up, and I'm living proof (as are the others out there like me—still living at home, doing very little but still dreaming big) that adolescence truly can be extended past the teen years.

Kidults are a tragic example of the Myth of Adolescence in action. And the consequences aren't limited to your teen years. After we shared Raymond's story at a conference in Indianapolis, a man (probably in his mid- to late forties) approached us. With tears in his eyes, he told us, "I'm Raymond. That story you told is exactly who I was."

He explained that he had done well in school when he was a teenager. His high school had a three-class structure for each grade, and he was in the top class every year. Because school was going so well, he thought he was free to party and experiment with drugs. But more than twenty years have passed, and he's *still* struggling with the repercussions.

"I thought the teen years were my time to party," he said. "And I've been paying the price ever since. I don't want teens today to make the same mistake."

The good news is, we don't have to! As we saw in the last chapter, what is considered "normal" today is actually a cruel exception—a myth. The teen years have *not* always been thought of as a time to waste, and teens haven't always been ripped off by low expectations. And there is hope, even for kidults. As we encouraged that man in Indianapolis: it's never too late to start doing hard things. William Wilberforce, one of the greatest rebelutionary examples who ever lived, wasted the first twenty-five years of his life on parties and social extravagance. And yet he went on to be the unrelenting force behind the abolition of slavery and emancipation of slaves throughout the British Empire.

How did he do it? First, God broke through and changed his heart. Immediately Wilberforce was filled with a profound sense of regret, bemoaning the "shapeless idleness" of his past and "the most valuable years of life wasted, and opportunities lost, which can never be recovered." But second, Wilberforce chose to do hard things. He threw himself into study and serious work. For over forty years he fought against slavery in the British Empire and, through his unwavering efforts, saw it abolished shortly before his death. Few men have left a greater mark on history.

This is the good news of the gospel. God offers grace and redemption to those with wasted pasts. But let us never presume upon God's grace by wasting even a minute of what Wilberforce rightly called "the most valuable years of life."

THE GENIUS OF HARD THINGS

Remember George, David, and Clara from the previous chapter? We left George as official surveyor of Culpeper County at age seventeen. David was in charge of a prize ship at age twelve, calmly keeping an unruly captain under control. Clara was nursing smallpox patients and overseeing a classroom of students at seventeen. Each of them clearly used their teen years to train and to launch. How did it serve them?

After three years as a surveyor in Virginia, the governor appointed George to the state militia as a major, a high rank. Then, when word came that the French were entering Ohio Territory, George was ordered to lead a midwinter expedition over hundreds of miles to assess their strength and to warn them to leave—which he successfully did.

By age twenty-two, George had been promoted to lieutenant colonel, and by age twenty-three, he was commander in chief of the entire Virginia militia. You might've heard about what he did later in life too. After twenty years, George became the commander in chief of the Continental army in the Revolutionary War, eventually becoming the first president of the United States—George Washington.

David's full name was David Farragut, the U.S. Navy's very first admiral and a hero during the Civil War. His courage in the face of heavy enemy fire in the Battle of Mobile Bay won him lasting fame—but it was far from his first act of bravery. He had been preparing for that moment ever since his childhood days as a cadet on the *Essex*.

Clara is best known as the founder of the American Red Cross—Clara Barton. Her desire to serve others started when she was eleven years old, caring for her brother David, and it only grew from there—to the sick in her village, to the children at the school where she taught, to thousands of wounded men in the Civil War, and later to millions through the American Red Cross.

There's a reason we still know the names and stories of men and women like George Washington, David Farragut, and Clara Barton. They invested their teen years in a way that shaped them into the history makers they later became.

You probably weren't surprised to hear how George, David, and Clara turned out. That's because all of us know that the teen years aren't some mystical period disconnected from the rest of our lives. For good or for bad, they will launch us into the future—our future.

In the stories of George, David, and Clara, we see that embracing responsibility and challenges in their teen years was genius. Why genius? Because doing hard things as teens prepared them for lives of incredible impact—lives that came with additional hard things that they wouldn't have been able to accomplish otherwise.

We need to be honest with ourselves. Is how we're spending our time right now preparing us for what we hope to become in the future? Are we doing things now that will equip us for the greater things God may have for us to do? These are the fundamental questions for this season of our lives.

A historian once said that George Washington "became the man he strove to be." That statement is not only true of Washington; it's also true about us. We will all become the men and women we strive (or don't strive) to be.

George, David, and Clara put into practice advice from the Old Testament: "It is good for a man that he bear the yoke in his youth" (Lamentations 3:27). As young people, they made a habit of overcoming obstacles—forging the determination and character that empowered them for the rest of their lives. Again, that shouldn't surprise us. After all, that's how effort works. That's the genius of choosing to do hard things.

Let's close off this chapter by looking at what we mean by "do hard things."

FIVE KINDS OF HARD

We call the following five categories the Five Kinds of Hard. They aren't secret, mystical, or helpful to just some—or even to just teens. They're God-given opportunities powered by God-given principles that work for everybody. If we launch into these opportunities now, we'll see powerful results—now and in our future. The examples we cite under each category are just that—examples. They are not intended to exhaustively define "hard things" for you, but rather give you a picture of the incredible variety of hard things available for us to do.

So here we go. Five different kinds of hard things:

1. Things that *are outside your comfort zone.* This could include activities like public speaking, learning a new skill or expanding an old one, traveling to new places, or meeting new people—anything that takes you outside the rut of your normal day-to-day, week-to-week activities. These actions can challenge us because they are unfamiliar or even scary, but they usually become some of our greatest memories, and they always end up growing our comfort zones for the future.

2. Things that *go beyond what is expected or required.*
   For example, say you only need a C to pass a class,
   but you aim for an A+. You aren't content to "do
   no harm"—you *purpose* to do good. You might
   volunteer to clean up after the church breakfast,
   stay late at work without pay to help a friend
   finish a job, or perform household chores you
   aren't even assigned. These actions are hard
   because they rest entirely on our own initiative.
   No one else will make us do them. Because of this,
   they are almost always the accomplishments we
   feel best about.

3. Things that *are too big to accomplish alone.* These are
   usually big projects like organizing a rally, making
   a film, forming a teen ministry to the homeless,
   changing your school's policy on a key issue, campaigning to get a shock jock off the air, or starting
   a band. They could also include *really* big causes like
   fighting modern-day slavery, abortion, or poverty
   and AIDS in Africa. We're passionate about these
   causes because God has placed them on our hearts.
   In order to be effective in these kinds of projects, we
   must be able to share our passion with others and
   recruit them to work alongside us.

4. Things that *don't earn an immediate payoff.* These are
   tasks like fighting sin, working out, doing your

schoolwork, and obeying your parents. They're hard because you won't see much progress from one day to the next and because, especially at the time, it can seem like you'd be happier if you didn't do them. Also, these are often tasks that no one else sees and that don't win you recognition or praise—things like being faithful in your spiritual disciplines, expending energy on good study habits, or driving the speed limit (even when you're late). We do them because they're right, not because they have an immediate payoff. In every case we'll be better off long-term, even though the things are "hard" or distasteful in the short-term.

5. Things that *challenge the cultural norm*. These choices go against the flow—dressing modestly, saying no to premarital sex, holding unpopular positions on issues like homosexuality and abortion, refusing to watch R-rated movies, sharing the gospel with others, or living as an obvious Christian. These choices are hard because they can cost you popularity and friendships. In some countries they can even cost you your life. In order to accomplish things in this category, we have to care more about pleasing God than we do about pleasing people around us. But the payoff is huge: if we do them, we can change the course of history.

Starting in the next chapter we'll be going in-depth with each of these categories. We'll help you overcome common obstacles that stand between you and the accomplishment of these hard things. And we'll show you how teens around the world are attempting and accomplishing hard and exciting things for God.

You'll meet a fifteen-year-old girl whose small idea launched an online project impacting thousands of people around the world; a fifteen-year-old guy who raised over twenty thousand dollars with a group of four friends to provide clean water for children in Africa; a nineteen-year-old who heads a Grammy-nominated band; and many other teens leading rebelutionary lives at home, at school, at church, and in their communities. These young people are rebelling against low expectations by choosing to get every possible benefit out of their teen years in creative, responsible, and highly effective ways.

As you read through the five categories, you probably thought of some hard things you've already done. If so, we're asking you to throw yourself into doing these things with a new level of passion because they are unique challenges God has prepared for you—because it's what you were made to do. We're asking you to live not your easiest life, but your best life according to God.

Five simple but power-packed choices help make that possible. That's what we're going to look at next.

PART 2

FIVE KINDS OF HARD

5

THAT FIRST
SCARY STEP

How to do hard things that take you outside your comfort zone

Meet a guy we know named Tyler. Tyler thought about graduating from high school early, but he wasn't sure if he could do it. So he didn't. After high school he had several ideas for business start-ups, but he didn't want to risk losing the little money he had if they went under. So he decided to wait. He considered going to college to study environmental engineering, but he was afraid he might change his mind partway through. So he stayed home.

Now Tyler is twenty-one years old, and he hasn't failed at anything. In fact, he hasn't really *done* anything. He's missed opportunity after opportunity to grow, explore, discover, and get stronger.

Life is full of scary things. You start your first day of high school. You deliver your first speech. You get married. Certain events mark important passages in our lives. Before the event you were one person. Afterward you are another. But Tyler has spent his life avoiding such firsts. The result? He's basically the same person he's always been.

This chapter is about doing hard things that take you from "before" to "after." We look especially at the step that makes important firsts possible—the one that takes you from the relative safety of your comfort zone to the scary territory outside it. Just thinking about taking a step like this makes many of us fret, fight, and freeze. We imagine that monsters of terror, shame, and pain will eat us alive. But if we do it anyway, we feel like celebrating.

We took that step just over two years ago—into "the new," leaving the old routines behind. Now, because of those experiences, we're different people; we've been transformed in ways that, sadly, Tyler has never experienced.

Doing hard things outside your comfort zone comes first in our list of five hard things that can start a rebelution in your life because—silly as it sounds—taking that first step outside your comfort zone is often the most terrifying "hard thing" of all. We also put it first because that first scary step is *always* necessary if we're going to attempt any of the other hard things we'll talk about later.

In our family, we like to reminisce (and laugh) about a huge step forward Brett took a little over ten years ago. He bravely fought, he flailed, he nearly drowned. But we should let Brett tell the story.

I still remember my first shower. It was a horrible experience. I was eight years old…

I didn't ask to be promoted from Junior Bath Taker
to First-Class Shower Taker, but one day my parents
realized, "He's eight years old. He's still taking baths!"
But baths were all I had ever known. Baths were neat
and tidy undertakings where the water flowed in safely
below my head and—provided I didn't splash too
much—stayed below my head and out of my eyes.

It didn't help that Alex loved showers.

Before I could object that day, I found myself wearing nothing but my birthday suit and staring up at that
dreadful showerhead. It pointed down at me like an

executioner's gun. Then Dad pulled the trigger, the shower began to rumble and hiss, and I was screaming before the first drop of water hit.

As scalding droplets stung my skin and water flooded my eyes, nose, and ears, I became convinced that my parents hated me. They couldn't possibly love me! What's more, I wasn't sure I loved them anymore either.

It's a good thing we lived out in the country. Otherwise the screams coming from the upstairs bathroom of the Harris home would have given neighbors reason to call 911. By the time Dad let me get out, I was a furious, miserable eight-year-old kid with soggy lungs.

But that was ten years ago. The funny thing is that this morning I took a shower and didn't think twice about it. The hot water felt good on my face. I didn't worry about drowning. I didn't hate anybody.

Isn't it incredible that what seemed so impossible when I was eight is now a vital, enjoyable part of my everyday routine?

We've All Had "First Shower" Experiences

The shower story is true. It's silly, but it illustrates a key point. Can you remember something in your own life that at the time seemed entirely beyond you? Maybe it was as simple as tying your shoes or riding a bike without training wheels. Maybe it was learning to read in kindergarten or solving basic math problems in second grade. At the time, each of these things was a major step outside your comfort zone. Today, of course, the same activities barely generate a yawn.

As silly as they may seem, each of those achievements proves something very important: If we take a step despite feeling uncomfortable, afraid, or inadequate, our comfort zones expand. We grow in strength and skill. What we consider normal for us changes, sometimes radically.

Take Jared for example. He took the step to fill in while his youth group's worship leader was away on a mission trip—even though he'd only been playing guitar for a few months. A year later he's leading worship for the entire church, and his band is looking to put out their first album. "That small step changed my entire direction," says Jared. "It opened the doors for me to do what I never thought possible."

The strange thing is that even when teens repeatedly experience the benefits of stepping outside our comfort zones, we tend to respond in exactly the same way to the next new task that comes along. We resist, delay, fight, and scream—all to keep from leaving our cozy little routines. But there's a high cost for choosing comfort; without even realizing it, we build an invisible fence around ourselves. Nothing challenging is allowed to enter—*even if it has the potential to set us free.* Inside the fence are all the things we feel comfortable attempting, things we've already done successfully. Outside the fence? Yikes!

Whenever we ask teens to list things outside their comfort zones, common fears come up: public speaking, attempting something new (especially if other people are watching or depending on you), traveling to new places, or meeting new people. These kinds of things seem hard because they're unfamiliar or even scary, but—have you noticed?—they usually end up generating our favorite stories and being some of our greatest memories.

In November 2007 we were invited to speak at two events in Japan, including a Christian teen conference in Tokyo. This was an incredible opportunity to minister to our generation in an entirely different part of the world. Even so, we were pretty nervous. Not only had we never really traveled outside the country before (we've been told that Canada doesn't count), we were also going to be speaking eight times—more than we'd ever done before. As if that wasn't far enough outside our comfort zones, we were going to be working with interpreters, which would be a completely new experience.

Almost everything about the trip was new and unknown—from the "strange" language to the "strange" toilets, to eating raw whale and squid. But in the end, though it definitely wasn't easy, it was nowhere near as difficult as we had imagined. Most important, the ministering that took place was amazing, and we formed incredible friendships with many people. Now we want to go back as soon as we can!

Looking back, the funny thing is that the hardest part of the trip was just deciding to go. Once we got into it we had a blast. But why is it that we can have such a hard time stepping outside of our comfort zones?

We've noticed that the fence that keeps us from breaking out of our comfort zones is nearly always built of fear—fear of weakness, discomfort, failure, humiliation. We've noticed something else too: you can't live by fear and live by faith at the same time. As Paul wrote in 2 Timothy 1:7, "God did not give us a spirit of timidity, but a spirit of power, of love and of self-discipline" (NIV). And when we read about the Bible heroes who accomplished big, hard things for God, we discover the main job requirement: "Without faith it is impossible to please God" (Hebrews 11:6, NIV).

Fortunately, fears are usually just well-concealed lies. In the next section we'll take a look at three powerful truths that can help you break through the fears that are holding you back from accomplishing hard things for God.

BREAKING OUT OF YOUR OLD ZONE

Think of each of the following three statements in this section as "zone breakers." Put these huge truths to work in your choices, and you'll understand why a comfort zone is actually a miserable place—and how you can escape yours.

1. God Works Through Our Weaknesses to Accomplish His Big Plans

Everyone likes to feel strong and smart. That means as soon as we start to feel stretched or pushed past our limits, we hit the brakes, slam into reverse, and scoot back to our comfort zones. Who wants to risk feeling weak and stupid?

Alyssa Chua, a seventeen-year-old rebelutionary from the Philippines, explained her pattern this way: "My comfort zone was the place where everything was just the way I wanted it to be; a situation where I never had to make extra effort or do something difficult; a place where I could sit back, relax, and enjoy myself."

The problem, she told us, was that when she stayed inside her comfort zone, she was essentially refusing to surrender her life fully to God; she was avoiding the hard things He was calling her to do.

Alyssa now realizes that stepping out of her comfort zone made all the difference. "Outside my comfort zone, I learned to lean on God for strength instead of leaning on the small pleasures of this world for comfort. Outside my comfort zone, I found that I could serve God more fully and use all of my talents unreservedly for Him."

We don't know about you, but we constantly find ourselves

building that invisible fence (the one that keeps threats out-side and us inside). We build it higher every time we say or think things like: "I'm just not a math person," "I'm just not organized—my brain doesn't work that way," or, "I'm just not a people person."

What we're really saying is that we don't want to do things that don't come easily or naturally. We don't want to break through our fears. And by our actions, we're also saying that God isn't good and powerful enough to help us do what we can't comfortably do on our own.

And that's a lie the Enemy loves! (He's read Hebrews 11:6 too.)

Smith Wigglesworth didn't learn to read until he was an adult, and he was unable to speak publicly for most of his life due to a terrible stammer. Against all odds he overcame this impediment and turned out to be one of England's greatest evangelists during his later years, leading thousands to Christ.

We could look at this story and say, "What a shame. If only speaking had come easily and early to him, think of how much more fruitful he could have been." But Wigglesworth recognized that the difficulties he overcame were vital to the effectiveness of his ministry. He liked to say, "Great faith is the product of great fights. Great testimonies are the outcome of great tests. Great triumphs can only come out of great trials."

So what are our reasons for sitting on our duffs and doing nothing?

1. We're not as good at something as someone else we know.
2. We don't have all the resources we think we need.
3. We figure that the chances of failing and looking like losers are too high.

But do you see the misconceptions hiding in all these reasons? We're really saying:

1. God only uses the best and brightest.
2. He only uses us when every last thing is in place.
3. He only brings glory to Himself when we...bring glory to ourselves too. (Ouch.)

Twelve-year-old Karen Kovaka wasn't a people person. She was the four-year-old who hid behind her mother at the mall, the seven-year-old who refused to come out from underneath her bed to meet dinner guests, and the twelve-year-old who burst into tears when she shook a stranger's hand.

Now her parents had registered her for a Communicators for Christ conference to help her overcome her fear of people. If Karen had known what attending this conference would actually require, she would've been terrified. As it turns out, she had no idea what she was getting into.

At that conference Karen began taking small steps outside her comfort zone and stumbled upon a revelation. "I not only learned how to give a speech," Karen tells us. "I also learned that shyness is a form of selfishness and that I had to overcome my fear of people if I actually wanted to live in the world and demonstrate compassion for others."

This first step into the realm of public speaking laid the foundation for a completely different future. From there her parents enrolled her in a national speech and debate league where she competed for four years. Her journey still included many tears, failures, and uncomfortable experiences, but she had learned that God's strength was greater than her weakness. She chose to compete in the most stretching categories, and by her fourth year she had earned nine national rankings.

But competitive success was not Karen's dream.

At the age of seventeen her dream came true when she was accepted to tour with Communicators for Christ, the same organization that had inspired her to leap beyond her limits five years earlier. Now eighteen, Karen is a personal assistant to the organization's executive director and helps train hundreds of young people to overcome their fear of public speaking and become communicators for Christ.

"It's amazing what youth can accomplish when they are awakened to what they can be, and have, at a young age," Karen says. "I think young people need to know that it's possible—that pursuing their dreams and goals isn't hopeless."

Karen feels that she is a living testimony to God's ability to cover our inadequacy with His sufficiency. "Young people want to do something significant, but they need to really believe that with God's help, they can."

It turns out that God loves to take stammering boys and shy girls and use them to change lives for eternity. And it's not about feeling strong; it's about obeying God.

Even when you're afraid.

2. Courage Is Not the Absence of Fear

Fear is the fence that keeps us stuck in our comfort zones. To be fair, we usually feel fear for a reason: often something *is* outside that should make us afraid. The problem is when we just sit there.

We wait.

And we wait.

Why? Well, we're waiting to stop feeling afraid before we attempt anything. And—just to be fair—we're often afraid to try something new because of painful past experiences. We tried stepping out before, and it blew up in our faces. We poured everything we had into something we cared about, and our efforts fell short. We don't want to embarrass ourselves again.

The truth, though, is that it's going to be a long wait. If we're waiting until the fear and feelings of inadequacy go away, we'll *never* venture outside our comfort zones. Until we take a step *in spite of our fears,* none of us will ever truly be able to do hard things. If we want to continue to grow and learn for the rest of our lives, we must beat these fears—not by making them go away, but by recognizing that there is something worse than discomfort, worse than the unknown, worse than failure. The worst thing is to never try at all.

Contrast the stories of Betsy and Grace:

"She's pregnant."

"I've never seen her before. Is she new?"

"I think so. I heard from my friend that she's pregnant. They're in the same class."

Betsy listened to her friends gossiping about the pregnant girl. She looked across the cafeteria. There she was, sitting all by herself. Alone. No one to talk to. To laugh with. To cry with.

I wonder what she's feeling right now, Betsy thought. *I wonder if she has a friend.* That's when Betsy felt it. The nudge.

Why now, God? Betsy thought. *Can't You find someone else to reach out to her? What will everyone think of me? I'm afraid!*

Go to her. The voice whispered again—loud and clear. Only Betsy didn't listen to the voice. Even though it told her the same thing for three days in a row.

After that the girl was gone.

"I'll always regret the way I ignored God's call to do what He told me to do," Betsy shared with us later. "I'll always wonder what she was like, how she ended up the way she was, and what could've happened if I'd talked with her."

Though Betsy knows that God has forgiven her, she is left asking, "What if?" What if she had chosen to obey God—despite her fear? How could her life—and the life of that girl—have been radically different?

One day last summer, nineteen-year-old Grace Mally promised God that she would witness to whomever she found at the park near her house—without turning back. But instead of a mom with a stroller, she found four burly construction workers repainting the merry-go-round.

What? Something must be wrong here. Surely God doesn't want me to witness to them! That would be so scary! Grace quickly turned around and started walking home. *Wait, no, I can't go home. I promised God that I was going to do this.* She slowly—very slowly—turned around and walked back to the park.

"I knew that I couldn't allow fear to take over," Grace recalls. "The Bible tells us so many times not to fear." Once she got started, her fear melted away entirely. The workers were surprisingly friendly, and she was able to be *double* good news—first by sharing the gospel and second by bringing them ice-cold lemonade.

"I don't know what the Lord was doing in the lives of the park maintenance crew," Grace says, "but I learned once again that if I allow fear to keep me from doing hard things, I'll miss out on the most exciting adventure life offers: obeying God."

Betsy and Grace: two girls and two different responses to God's calling.

Our father often tells us, "True courage is not the absence of fear. It is refusing to allow fear to control your actions." Grace's courage showed up in the fact that she committed to obeying God—regardless of how she felt. Betsy was held captive by her fear and chained down by feelings of inadequacy.

But not the next time.

"I now know that God wasn't asking me to do it on my own," Betsy says. "He was simply calling me to follow His direction and see what would happen. He wanted me to draw my confidence from Him."

Of course, we're not encouraging you to go jump into an aquarium with a bunch of sharks—some fears are healthy! Instead we're talking about things you know you *should* do but *aren't* doing because you're afraid you might fail, afraid you'll feel awkward or foolish, or just afraid of the new and unknown.

Overcoming our fears doesn't require that we stop caring about what happens. It just requires that we act in spite of our fear. Slavery to fear is much worse than the bruises and scars of a few falls. Letting fear control your actions is a statement of distrust in the goodness of God. If we allow fear to paralyze us, we'll look back at our life with remorse for all the times we could have and should have—but did not.

The good news is that all it takes to overcome many of our fears is to face them—with God's help—by taking the first step. The first step is always the hardest.

3. You Can't Get to Success Without Risking Failure

We all like to win. It sure beats losing. But a very promising competitive streak can also breed a very limiting dread of failure. *If I do this and fail,* we tell ourselves, *disaster will follow and everyone will know I'm a loser.*

Do you see the all-or-nothing fallacy in that line of thinking? The choice is win…or disaster. But the truth in this area is so liberating. Unless we're being intentionally foolish, a failure is never total. We aren't called to be successful all the time. We're called to be faithful, to take those first difficult steps— and to leave the results up to God.

Fourteen-year-old Caleb had wanted to record a CD for years. He'd finally saved up enough money to buy the equipment he needed and had transformed his bedroom into a studio. Now he just needed to learn how the equipment worked.

He decided to learn by doing.

It took Caleb three weeks to record two songs and three more weeks of spinning dials and punching buttons to finish editing. This wasn't six weeks off and on; this was six weeks of every spare minute. He made dozens (and dozens) of mistakes trying to learn the equipment and once had to start over completely after he thought he was finished. For all this work, he sold three CDs. Not counting grandparents, he sold one.

At times like these we need to remember that anything worth doing is worth doing poorly—at first. Anything worth doing is worth failing at and trying again. The Bible says that the righteous man falls seven times and gets back up again (Proverbs 24:16).

Interestingly enough, the other time the Bible references doing something seven times (forgiving others), Jesus clarifies that seven times might as well mean seventy times seven. Have any of us ever failed and then tried again at something 490 times? For that matter, have any of us ever tried even seven times?

Caleb's failure could have discouraged him from ever trying again. It was the kind of fiasco that seemed to say, "You have a brighter future sticking with PlayStation." But Caleb didn't see it that way. He was excited he had learned to use the equipment!

Since that first attempt Caleb has completed several larger projects—all in a fraction of the time. Having mastered the technical side of recording and mixing, he's able to focus on improving his guitar playing and songwriting. Plus, now that Caleb's friends are aware he has an in-house studio and knows how to use it, they're bringing their instruments over and jamming with him.

"It's a lot better than when I was trying to play every instrument myself." Caleb laughs. "I'm pretty sure we're going to start a band this summer. I'm pretty stoked."

What Caleb learned is that it's okay to fail at hard things, because all effort—even failed effort—produces growth.

For example, we were once with a large group of guys when someone had the brilliant idea of holding a push-up contest. The goal was a hundred push-ups. Most of the guys wouldn't even attempt it—either because they were afraid they might fail or because they *knew* they would. In the end two or three guys who knew they could reach a hundred, and Brett and Alex, who knew we *couldn't* reach a hundred, actually embarked on this extremely masculine endeavor.

The outcome was no surprise. We lost—badly. In the end we were lying there on the floor, unable to get up, thinking, *That was such a stupid idea. What were we thinking? Will we ever be able to get up again?*

Here's where a "do hard things" mentality comes in: we probably got a better workout than the other guys did. Think about it. They exerted themselves—until they won. Then they stopped. We exerted ourselves too. But we stretched. We pushed ourselves to our limits and beyond. We got stronger even though we failed to hit the goal.

So many of us allow little failures to keep us from gaining important skills, from maintaining vital relationships, or even from accomplishing great things in our lives. A "do hard things" perspective reminds us that all effort—even failed effort—builds muscle. It tells us that the reason we can't do a hundred push-ups is because we haven't built up the strength with consistent exercise. It turns failure on its head, making it work for us rather than against us. It makes failure a way to grow stronger, not a reason to give up.

A Step into the Unknown

Brothers Seth and Ian Willard were eighteen and sixteen respectively. Neither of them had done any political campaigning before. However, they'd just attended a conference where one of the speakers challenged students to make a difference in the political process. And guess what? It was an election year.

"At that point we had a decision to make," Ian recalls. "We could either sit back and watch, or we could hop in and risk making fools of ourselves."

Back home in Minnesota they decided to take a simple step of faith and call one of the candidates they supported to offer their services. "We were really nervous before we made the call," admits Seth, "but he was very happy to hear from us, and it turned out he could use plenty of help." The next Saturday the brothers were out working on his state senate campaign.

Less than a week later Seth and Ian heard that one of their family's old church friends was running for county sheriff. Once again they offered their services, and once again they were invited to attend his first campaign meeting. Before they knew what was happening, they were members of his campaign board. And Ian wasn't even old enough to vote!

Seth and Ian recruited many of their friends to work alongside them, and word about their team spread. They started getting calls from other campaigns asking for help. Eventually they found themselves traveling across the state to work on a national election for the U.S. Congress. A few weeks later they watched with satisfaction as the results came in. All of the campaigns they'd worked on were successful.

With these victories under their belts, it was hard to believe that just a few months earlier they'd never done this before and weren't sure where to start.

"At first I was tempted to swell up with pride because I had saved America," says Ian, laughing. "But then I realized that it has nothing to do with me. I was merely a tool in God's hands. It's humbling that He used me to accomplish what He wanted to do."

We love Seth and Ian's story because it so clearly demonstrates the three "zone breakers" we've looked at in this chapter:

1. We see God working through them, despite their inexperience, to accomplish big things.
2. We see them acting in spite of their fear. They took

> the first step of making a phone call, and God
> opened a floodgate of opportunities.
> 3. We see them risk failing and looking foolish, and as a
>   result, they find success and vision for the future.

Since this experience, both Seth and Ian have felt called to encourage the rest of their generation to get involved. Stepping outside of their comfort zones once again, they've started a local club that brings elected officials to speak to students and leads groups to the state capitol to meet with their representatives and watch the senate in session.

"Our story started with a simple step into the unknown," says Seth, "but by God's grace our story has only just begun. We can't wait to see what comes next."

UNKNOWN FUTURE, KNOWN GOD

An interesting map is on display in the British Museum in London. It's an old mariner's chart, drawn in 1525, outlining the North American coastline and adjacent waters. The cartographer made some intriguing notations on areas of the map that represented regions not yet explored. He wrote, "Here be giants," "Here be fiery scorpions," and "Here be dragons." Fortunately, explorers ignored his warnings—and discovered whole new continents as a result!

In this chapter we've seen that it's not the giants, fiery scorpions, and dragons that keep us behind our fences. It's the *fear* of them. Once we take that first scary step with God's help—and keep going forward—we'll actually experience the bigger, more fulfilling life God has in mind for us.

Not only that, but we have seen that God is ready to work through us, even with our limitations, and bless our failures. Instead of worrying about future fears, we can, as Corrie ten Boom wrote, "Never be afraid to trust an unknown future to a known God."

It's been nearly a decade since Brett's first shower, one of the great challenges of his childhood. Since then he's tackled a lot of new tasks—some almost as fearsome as getting water in his eyes and ears. "When I find myself thinking that these new challenges are going to kill me," he says, "I just remember that I thought the same thing about my first shower. Then I smile and keep on pushing."

What if the same could be said about the enormous challenges you face today? Take a moment to ponder the following questions:

- What could your life look like if your trust in God overcame your fears?
- How could your life be different if you chose to do hard things by stepping outside your comfort zone?

The stories we've shared in this chapter are just examples of a reality that has been proven true in thousands of lives. What if a kid who suffers from severe anxiety attacks could go on to be a fifteen-year-old who has spoken to over half a million people at live events, appeared on national television numerous times, and even delivered speeches at the White House? Not possible?

His name is Zach. And anything is possible with God.

Throughout the rest of this book we'll introduce you to dozens more young people, including Zach, whose lives have been transformed by surrendering themselves to God and following wherever He leads—even when it takes them way outside their comfort zones.

To hear them tell it, that's where the very best things happen.

6

RAISING THE BAR

How to do hard things that go beyond what's expected or required

Sarah, a nineteen-year-old sophomore at Olympic College in Washington, vividly recalls the day she received her worst grade ever on an English paper. It came back from the teacher covered with scribbled comments. At the end the teacher had added a devastating note—and an opportunity. The note said this: *There is much room for improvement, Sarah, should you choose to revise.*

Surprisingly, it wasn't the grade that hurt. Not at all, Sarah says. It was something much bigger: a painful realization that she had been sliding by, measuring her work only by the grades and not by more important criteria like, *Have I done my best?* or, *Am I actually learning?*

Sarah sheepishly told us, "I'd written papers before and knew that they showed a lack of understanding, and yet I still made good grades." But her English professor saw that Sarah was getting by with little effort. "She had read my paper carefully and identified what was lacking. But she'd also seen my potential."

How did Sarah fall into the rut of delivering only the bare minimum in her classes?

"When I first got to school, I actually felt relieved by the low expectations," Sarah explained. "I could hold down my job, do the minimum amount of homework, and still make good grades." But it had come at a cost. She'd become complacent.

As painful as the experience was, Sarah is still grateful that one professor saw through her game—and raised the bar.

Sarah accepted the challenge and chose to revise. At first she doubted her ability, but after a few hours of reworking, she realized her new draft was really improved. "Once I revised my paper and saw how much better I did when challenged, the light went on. I realized that I hadn't actually been learning anything before."

That day Sarah realized that if she truly wanted to be prepared for life, she'd have to take responsibility for her own education. If she measured success only by other people's standards of what was acceptable, she would never reach her true potential. She would need to set her own bar high and then do her best to exceed it.

"You'd think that just doing an assignment and fulfilling a professor's expectations would produce a quality learning experience," she said. "But in my case it didn't. After a year at college and ten professors, I've realized that at least half of them didn't expect enough of me."

THE TRAP OF "JUST DO YOUR BEST"

Can you relate to Sarah's story? It's easy to be content with less than our best, especially when our halfhearted efforts seem to satisfy everyone around us. And being "good enough" can turn into a special hazard. Those who could do *a lot better* or tackle a *much bigger challenge* seldom do so when they're already "good enough" by other people's standards.

What about you? Maybe you've procrastinated on a school project because you knew you could stay up late the night before the deadline and throw something together. Or maybe you've accepted your place in the middle of the pack even though you know that's not where you belong. In many ways you can deliver less than 100 percent and still get away with it—on a team, in youth group, at work, at home, in your personal and spiritual life.

In this chapter, we'll look at one of the most important but challenging steps you can take to beat the tide of low expectations: reject complacency and choose to do hard things that go above and beyond what's required or expected of you.

This choice goes right to the heart of what it means to be a rebelutionary. Without a doubt, pushing yourself to do more than is asked, expected, or required is nearly always a lonely choice. It can set you apart from friends, co-workers, other Christians, even family. As we'll see, the desire to do your best—even when no one around you requires it—takes a special kind of character. It puts you at odds with the accepted culture, which says "Just do your best" but means something very different.

Think about it. This common phrase, "Just do your best," actually encourages the opposite. When someone says, "Just do your best," are you inspired to reach for more? Or does it feel like permission to just get by? We say, "Hey, I did my best." But did we really? More likely what we mean is, "Hey, I gave it a shot, and that'll have to be good enough."

Believe it or not, the "good enough" and "just do your best" mind-sets actually stem from the enemy we met in the second chapter: the Myth of Adolescence.

Meet Mr. Complacency

The Myth of Adolescence tries to get you in one of two ways. The first is to flat-out brainwash you with low expectations. If that doesn't work, it happily paints you as an exception. In this case, being an exception means that compared to the irresponsibility, immaturity, and incompetence expected from teenagers, you are officially "above average."

Wow! A gold star for you!

But wait a minute. Being labeled an exception when you're barely even trying quickly turns into a trap of its own. You can become like Sarah, floating along on your above-average status in a river of meager requirements. Your gold star reduces the chances that you'll ever live up to your actual potential.

Before long you'll become blinded by complacency, which is defined as a smug feeling of satisfaction with who you are and what you've done. Recognize that feeling? We do. We *like* that feeling, honestly. But we're learning that smug satisfaction leads to genuine disappointment before long.

Here's why. Like pride, complacency thrives when hidden behind rationalizations ("Hey, I did my best..."). Obviously this means that the majority of complacent people don't think they have a problem. And as many wise men throughout history have observed, the most dangerous enemy is the one we fail to recognize. Since you don't think you have a problem—How could you? You're above average!—you're an easy victim for a lot of sweet-sounding lies.

Imagine if complacency were a person in your life. Mr. Complacency would come up beside you, admire that shiny gold star of yours, and then whisper smugness-inducing flattery like:

- "People think you're so great. Lucky you—you've got it made without even trying."
- "Everything is going just fine. Why accept a new challenge where you might fail?"
- "You're okay just the way you are. Why work to improve yourself?"
- "Compared to some people—*cough*—you're not *that* bad!"
- "From what I hear, Thomas Edison and Bill Gates never got a gold star."

Listen to Mr. Complacency long enough and he'll convince you that what you really, really need is a nap.

But don't kid yourself. The cost of complacency is real, and it can be tragic. We slide into habits of mediocrity and excuse making. Life gets boring, and we're not sure why. We know, or at least suspect, that there's a lot more we could do or be. But floating along, there's no way to be sure. Might as well take another nap.

The daily periodical *Bits & Pieces* shares this chilling picture of what's really happening:

Complacency is a blight that saps energy, dulls attitudes, and causes a drain on the brain. The first symptom is satisfaction with things as they are. The second
is rejection of things as they might be. "Good enough"
becomes today's watchword and tomorrow's standard.

Complacency makes people fear the unknown,
mistrust the untried, and abhor the new. Like water,
complacent people follow the easiest course—downhill.
They draw false strength from looking back.

Proverbs 1:32 is even clearer: "The complacency of fools
destroys them."

Over time, refusing to reach higher, try harder, and risk
more robs us of the glorious purpose and wonderful future
God has created us for.

If we're fortunate, one day we'll get a wake-up call like
Sarah's—a jolt that makes us see how our real life is drifting
by—and we'll decide to reach for more.

Hopefully a *lot* more.

Three Strategies for Stepping Higher

We recommend that rebelutionaries do three hard things that
go above and beyond what our culture expects and take us
closer to what God expects:

1. Do what's hard for you.

2. Be known for what you do (more than for what you don't).

3. Pursue excellence, not excuses.

Do What's Hard for You

Remember Heidi, the county campaign coordinator in our Alabama Supreme Court race? She jumped into something that, for her, was terrifying—talking on the phone, especially to strangers. For a lot of teens, being on the phone is like breathing or eating pizza: can't do without it, don't think much about it when it's happening. But not for Heidi. That's what we mean here when we say do what's hard *for you*. A rebelutionary takes the time to identify the areas where he or she could accomplish more by stepping across the line of what comes easily and coming out from behind past accomplishments, complacency, and low expectations.

Mark is homeschooled, but he plays basketball with the varsity team at the local high school. Mark is one of the top scorers in the division, and basketball has been his life ever since he can remember. He spends hours at the gym almost every day, not including official practices, shooting hundreds of free throws, running drills, and extending the range of his jump shot. If you ask anyone who knows Mark whether he does hard things, they'll say yes—and Mark knows it. But the truth is, he uses his athletic reputation as an excuse to not spend as much time on a lot of things that don't come as naturally to him—like reading difficult books and helping his family out around the house.

If Mark were honest with himself, he'd admit that he has allowed other important areas of his life to drift too low on his priority list or has even dismissed them entirely. All of us have the tendency to emphasize our strong points and then use them as an excuse to neglect our weaker points—and that's Mark's game. We would all like to pick just the strongest areas of our lives and say, "This is me. Ignore everything else. This is who I am." But if we want to live as rebelutionaries, we can't afford that luxury.

Take Heather, another teen we met during the Alabama campaigns. All she wanted people to see was her leadership position in a national youth organization. As a gifted young person in a culture of low expectations, Heather could easily stand out and gain attention for doing relatively little compared to her potential. Since most people were impressed with her, she had become pretty impressed with herself.

"I started reading your blog," Heather wrote us a few months after we'd returned home to Oregon. "One of the first things that caught my attention was your emphasis on not becoming complacent in our 'excellence'—that it's not enough to impress a society with remarkably low expectations; it's not enough to be a standout in a sea of mediocrity."

With this realization, Heather began to focus, not on things that were impressive to others, but on things that actually challenged her and caused her to grow. For Heather this meant focusing on reaching out to others and being faithful in the small things not many people see. The rest of her letter is a beautiful example of how doing what's hard for you can pull you out of complacency and spark radical growth:

> I began to focus on doing harder things than I had ever done before. I refocused on mentorship and "how we may spur one another on toward love and good deeds" (Hebrews 10:24, NIV). I changed my password on my work computer to a variation of "do hard things" as a daily reminder to start the day brainstorming for at least one comfort zone–stretching thing I could do.
>
> In the midst of these changes, I also read John Piper's book *Don't Waste Your Life*. My thoughts throughout the day would take the shape of the question, *What hard thing can I do today that will have an eternal impact for the sake of the gospel?*
>
> One answer the Lord gave me was to start a monthly e-newsletter for [the] office where I work. It will include announcements, birthday recognitions, recipes, jokes, holiday celebration ideas, and a bold presentation of the gospel. I've also had the opportunity to give a clear presentation of the gospel to two of my co-workers.

At church I've been personally reaching out to people that I wouldn't have reached out to otherwise, and when I talk to my friends, I've been trying to direct the conversation to more substantial matters. At home I've sought to do hard things—even things as simple as staying calm when before I would have gotten upset, or volunteering for an extra task around the house.

Has "do hard things" changed my life? Yes, it has. The Lord has used the Rebelution to jolt me out of my complacent self-satisfaction and give me a new vision for what it means to inspire others to excellence in Christ.

Be Known for What You Do (More than for What You Don't)

Lindsey is in her second year of high school—her first at a private Christian school. Even among other Christian teens at school and church, Lindsey is the "good girl" who seemingly never does anything wrong. She won't watch R-rated movies, wears a promise ring her dad gave her on her thirteenth birthday, and won't even date (or "court," as she puts it) until she's ready to get married. It doesn't make her highly popular among some of her peers, but she cares more about what the adults in her life think. And they praise her constantly—usually while they bemoan all the "bad stuff" other teens today are involved in.

She loves it when she gets compliments for being such a "wonderful girl," but when Lindsey is honest, she knows she's become exceptional for what she *doesn't* do. She doesn't attend wild parties, cause trouble, or want a tattoo. But what does she *do*? Is the Christian life all about avoiding "bad stuff" or is it about doing "good, hard stuff" for God? Deep down Lindsey knows the answer, but she's already praised for being such a godly girl. Isn't that enough?

Bre, a high-school senior from Indiana, experienced low expectations firsthand. She, along with other young people, had participated in some community service projects and afterward gave a report to her church. Following the service she overheard a man saying, "Aren't you glad these kids aren't out smoking pot or drinking?"

"That comment just broke my heart," Bre wrote to us, "because there truly is a level of mediocrity that has infiltrated not just our culture, but our churches as well." Being considered a good teen only requires that we don't do bad stuff like taking drugs, drinking, and partying. But is it enough to be known for the negative things we don't do, or should we also be known for the positive and difficult things that we *do*?

God's Word is clear. Our culture's standard of simply not doing bad stuff is really no standard at all. Psalm 1:1 tells us, "Blessed is the man who walks not in the counsel of the wicked, nor stands in the way of sinners, nor sits in the seat of scoffers." A lot of people, though, seem to quit reading there and miss the next verse: "But his delight is in the law of the LORD, and on his law he meditates day and night."

Our culture seems to hear the don'ts but miss the dos.

Charles Spurgeon, the great preacher of the nineteenth century, commented, "Perhaps some of you can claim a sort of negative purity, because you do not walk in the way of the ungodly; but let me ask you—Is your delight in the law of God? Do you study God's Word? Do you make it the man of your right hand—your best companion and hourly guide?" If not, Spurgeon said, the blessing of Psalm 1 does not belong to you.

To live by God's standards for young people and to enjoy the blessing He promises, we must get beyond simply avoiding bad stuff. To see this we need only look at the theme verse of the Rebelution, 1 Timothy 4:12: "Don't let anyone look down on you because you are young, but set an example for the believers in speech, in life, in love, in faith and in purity" (NIV). We're not just supposed to avoid sinning; we're supposed to pursue righteousness in a way that others will want to imitate.

Jason, a twentysomething from Florida, understands this principle well. He e-mailed us shortly after we started our blog and explained that he'd recently grown complacent with his life, just working his job and getting by. "Not that a steady working life isn't God's plan for some," Jason said, "but I was feeling empty and knew that God had more abundant plans for me. I knew He had some hard things for me to do."

Jason realized that though he wasn't headed in the wrong

direction, he wasn't exactly headed in the right direction either. He told us that now he's planning to switch gears and attend law school with the goal of advocating for pro-life groups.

For Jason, doing hard things meant pursuing challenges that would cause him to grow. It meant going beyond what others required of him so he could become more effective in the Lord's service. He wasn't content to merely survive; he wanted to thrive.

Pursue Excellence, Not Excuses

Mary is a junior in high school. A strong Christian, she proudly puts to rest the idea that Christians are stupid and unpopular by being head of her class and co-captain of the cheerleading squad. Her parents, teachers, and youth pastor all have big plans for her, and Mary has big plans for herself. But because things come easily for her, she's become comfortable with her "standout" status. She doesn't have to tell herself she's great because other people will do it for her, even when she hasn't done anything particularly difficult. She's above average without even trying, so she sees no reason to push herself.

Mary has fallen prey to the curse that low expectations place on talented people. She has gotten stuck doing what comes easily because even things that are easy for her are impressive to others. In her mind, she has already arrived—yet she has never explored the true extent of her potential.

Shortly after we started The Rebelution blog, we received the following letter, which addresses the complacency Mary has slipped into and then points the way out:

> The real danger for youths intent on rebelution is that these smarter-than-the-average-bear kudos can become the new and easy standard.
>
> Unfortunately, we often get praise for things that weren't particularly difficult to achieve. If we focus on the props and the encouragement of those who have low expectations for us, we become mediocre.
>
> It can be challenging to set our sights on excellence, particularly when we're hearing that we're already there. One of life's greatest lessons, which we all must learn, could be expressed in the phrase "That was nothing. Watch this." Challenge yourself and others to call the normal things *normal* and save that word *excellent* for things that really are.

Since we got this letter, we've received several others from teens complaining about getting corny awards at school like the Celebration of Excellence for Leadership. All they'd done was turn in their homework and pay attention in class while everyone else goofed off. "It's sad how little I had to do to earn this award," wrote one girl.

Just like Mary, we can get so caught up in being the god-liest person in our youth group or in earning the Celebration of Excellence for Leadership award that we lose sight of God's standards. We fall short of our true potential because we aimed only to be bigger than the next fish in our small pond.

The students who have written to us recognized this and weren't about to hijack their futures just because they'd managed to exceed mediocre standards. They realized that God's standard is not for us to be the godliest person in a youth group filled with halfhearted Christians, but to "be holy" because He is holy (1 Peter 1:16). God's standard is not for us to be our teacher's best helper, but to be a "servant of all" (Mark 9:35).

God set His standards this high so that we won't make the mistake of aiming low. He made them unreachable so that we would never have an excuse to stop growing.

We can identify complacency in our lives by asking ourselves the following hard questions and then answering them honestly:

- *What areas of my life do I not care about that I know I should care about?*
- *In what areas have I fallen short of God's standards and my own potential?*
- *In what areas have I settled for just getting by when I know I could do better if I really tried?*

- *In what areas have I decided that things "will always be this way" without ever putting in the kind of effort that really changes things?*

These questions are difficult because no one else can answer them for you. Only you know how much better you could be if you really tried, and if you've never really tried, then even you might not know.

Take Wenslyn Reyes for example. Ever since she was little, she's been involved in the ministry of the Chinese/English church she attends in the Philippines. Now eighteen, Wenslyn is the youngest worship pianist, the youngest pulpit translator, and the youngest study group leader in the church. Everyone considers her somewhat of a prodigy, and she is praised constantly.

"I may not be the best translator or accompanist I could be," Wenslyn writes us, "but I am so good *for my age*—as everyone likes to put it—that I'm often tempted to be content with my 'prodigy' status."

The "do hard things" message has challenged Wenslyn to become a better steward of her talents by exploring her full potential. She now realizes that God has allowed her to start ministry early so that she can go further in the long run. Instead of just aiming to be "good for her age," Wenslyn has committed to improving herself to be all God has gifted her to be.

"'Do hard things' means fighting for greater levels of excellence because there is always something harder to do," she writes us. "It is never a matter of arriving; it is a constant battle for growth."

Complacency is rendered helpless when confronted with this kind of mind-set, because it depends on us losing steam, becoming satisfied, and feeling as if we have already arrived. Wenslyn's goal is growth—not just impressing other people.

A commitment to growth kills complacency.

For another strong shot of inspiration, jump back with us a hundred and fifty years to the story of a young man who didn't seem to have much going for him *except* mediocrity and limitations. Then—like Sarah, Heather, Jason, and Wenslyn—he decided to rethink what he'd been considering good enough and reach for something more.

The world is still benefiting from what happened next.

FROM WIMP TO WORLD-CHANGER

As a young teenager, Theodore Roosevelt didn't strike anyone as the kind of person who would become one of America's greatest presidents. From the time he was a toddler, severe asthma overshadowed everything he did. He was considered too delicate for school and too weak to stand up to other boys. On doctor's orders his father and mother rushed him to seashore resorts and mountain cabins in hopes that changes of air would help him breathe. The sickly boy seemed unlikely to survive childhood—let alone amount to anything if he did.

Of course, we all know that Theodore "Teddy" Roosevelt did more than survive. In a way that few men have matched, he thrived. In the eyes of his fellow Americans, he went on to reach the stature of George Washington, Thomas Jefferson, and Abraham Lincoln, his face forever immortalized with theirs on the side of Mount Rushmore.

More than any of his contemporaries, Roosevelt led America into the twentieth century. He was a cowboy on the western frontier, a police commissioner in New York City, a military hero in the Spanish-American War, and the governor of New York. He was the first president to fly in an airplane, to be submerged in a submarine, to have a telephone in his home, or to own a car. He was the first president to champion conservation and pass laws to protect the environment. He was the first president to leave American soil while in office. And in 1906 he became the first American Nobel laureate, awarded the Nobel peace prize for almost single-handedly negotiating a peaceful end to the Russo-Japanese War.

How did a severely nearsighted, asthmatic kid who wasn't expected to live past his twenty-first birthday go on to experience a life of such incredible accomplishment? The short answer is that as a teenager, Roosevelt chose to go beyond what was easy by reaching for what seemed impossible.

Shortly before his twelfth birthday, his father took him aside and challenged him to dedicate himself to the "hard drudgery" of building himself a strong body. Convinced and determined, young Roosevelt gave himself to it, spending hours each day lifting weights, hammering punching bags, and straining at pull-up bars. His sisters would later write that one of their most vivid childhood memories was the sight of their brother struggling between the horizontal bars, "widening his chest by regular, monotonous motion—drudgery indeed."

This was the beginning of the transformation—more than just physical—that would shape the rest of his life. Decades later, with conviction birthed in the "hard drudgery" of his teen years, Roosevelt said that the highest form of success would go only to the man who "does not shrink from danger, from hardship, or from bitter toil."

Theodore Roosevelt learned the most important lesson of his life as a teenager. It was a lesson that informed and made possible everything he did from that point on: "do hard things." Listen to what he said about what he called "the strenuous life":

I wish to preach, not the doctrine of ignoble ease, but the doctrine of the strenuous life, the life of effort, of labor and strife; to preach that highest form of success which comes, not to the man who desires mere easy peace, but to the man who does not shrink from danger, from hardship, or from bitter toil, and who out of these wins the splendid ultimate triumph.

Of course, nowadays we don't talk the way Roosevelt did. But what would happen if we embraced the values he did—of reaching above and beyond what comes easy? And what would happen if a new generation of teens lived that way?

Start now.

7

THE POWER
OF COLLABORATION

How to do hard things that
are too big for you to do alone

As long as Kelsey* can remember, she's been interested in anything to do with clothing. She's sixteen now, but even when she was four years old, she would watch old movies with plots way over her head just because she liked to look at the beautiful costumes. She wants to go into fashion

---

* This name has been changed.

107

design when she grows up. But here's the catch: she wants it to be with a fashion company that values *modesty*.

Her fascination with what she describes as the "forgotten quality" of modesty grew out of her love for fashion—that and many late-night mother-daughter talks as she was entering her teen years. "My desire to dress well expanded into a desire to please God by how I dress," she told us. "And thus began my quest to figure out what modesty is. In my reading I always found very good reasons why to dress modestly. But everything I read seemed to leave out the important detail of what *modest* means."

She knew that modesty was a heart issue, but it was also a clothing issue. She was puzzled by the lack of resources, and she was especially frustrated that nothing she found presented views on modesty from Christian guys' point of view.

Kelsey was sure that other girls had a lot of the same questions she did, but she didn't know where to turn for answers. She had an idea that someday she'd find some godly Christian guys who would allow her to ask questions about modesty and would give answers she could share with other girls. But how and when and where? Should she just stand in the church lobby with a clipboard?

Kelsey felt strongly that she was wrestling with important issues. *How do Christian guys really feel about the way girls dress? What is modest to a guy?* She thought if she could get solid answers, she could help thousands of teenagers. But she didn't know how or where to start.

Her challenge was simply too big for one girl to figure out.

If you've ever had an idea that you felt was just too big for you or been faced with a project where you didn't even know where to start, you probably know how Kelsey felt. Some hard things are too big to be accomplished alone. We call them "big hard things," and responding correctly when faced with them is what this chapter is all about.

Big hard things range from Kelsey's quest to things like organizing an event at your church or school, making a film, reaching out to the homeless in your community, campaigning to get a crude TV show off the air in your community, or starting a band. Big hard things can also include *really* big causes—fighting to end modern-day slavery, abortion, poverty, or AIDS. We'll be taking a closer look at those kinds of big hard things in chapters 10 and 11.

Unfortunately, more than any other kind of hard thing we talk about in this book, the response to big hard things is usually to give up before we even try. *It's too big for me, end of story,* we tell ourselves.

We need to change the way we think about large projects and big ideas. Instead of focusing on our individual limitations, what if we stepped back, looked around, and asked, "Who could be motivated to tackle this *with* me?" The answer to that question, as you'll see in this chapter, makes possible a whole new range of options for rebelutionaries. The answer is collaboration—one of the three pillars of the Rebelution.

Notice the parts *co* and *labor* in that word? They give you a picture of what collaboration is—literally "working together."

STRENGTH IN NUMBERS

American popular lore tries to persuade us that our destiny was won only by rugged individuals who stood tall, acted alone, rarely talked, and drank their whiskey straight. We're taught to admire the rebel, the loner, the maverick. But the facts suggest that the achievements of nations—like those of corporations, armies, universities, sports teams, churches, and families—depend heavily on people coming together to co-labor: to agree on a common goal and then collaborate to make it happen.

Who we collaborate with, of course, is a big deal. Throughout the Bible, we're taught to make sure we're doing the right things *with the right people*. For example, in 2 Timothy 2:22, Paul instructs us to "flee youthful passions and pursue righteousness, faith, love, and peace, *along with those* who call on the Lord from a pure heart."

We love that verse because it captures the rebelutionary

mind-set of collaboration: rebelling against low expectations ("flee youthful passions"), doing hard things ("pursue [or strive after]"), and harnessing the power of teamwork (*along with those* who call on the Lord from a pure heart").

A study of horses revealed that a single horse could pull an average of 2,500 pounds. The test was repeated with two horses. You'd expect the weight pulled to double—to about 5,000 pounds. Not so. Two horses working together pulled *12,500 pounds!* That's *five times* the amount one could pull alone.

Would the numbers hold if instead of horses researchers had used Vespas or Volkswagens? We doubt it. There's something inside a living being that rises to accomplish exponentially greater things when part of a team.

God has made all of us (not just horses) to be more effective when we work in fellowship with others. In fact, the Bible warns us of the danger of isolating ourselves from others. Hebrews 10:24–25 says, "Let us consider how to stir up one another to love and good works, not neglecting to meet together, as is the habit of some, but encouraging one another." Proverbs 18:1 is even more blunt: "Whoever isolates himself seeks his own desire; he breaks out against all sound judgment."

People who try to just "go it alone" miss out on the relational advantages as well. Ecclesiastes 4:9–12 tells us:

Two are better than one, because they have a good
reward for their toil. For if they fall, one will lift up
his fellow. But woe to him who is alone when he falls
and has not another to lift him up! Again, if two lie
together, they keep warm, but how can one keep warm
alone? And though a man might prevail against one
who is alone, two will withstand him—a threefold
cord is not quickly broken.

When he was seventeen, Jeremy Blaschke and his home-
school group decided to raise money to buy an ultrasound
machine for a crisis pregnancy center. Looking back, he says
he didn't really know what he was getting into.

"I'd never paid that much for anything before," he told us,
referring to the ultrasound machine's twenty-five-thousand-
dollar price tag. "I didn't have a grasp of how much that actually was and what it meant to say we were going to raise it."

After a big fund-raiser at the local fair and another at
Jeremy's church, they had raised thirty-two hundred dollars
toward their goal—and spirits were high. "At the time I was
thinking that it was going to be easy, that we could get it done
in a few months," Jeremy said.

Instead it got harder. Spring turned to summer—and
summer to fall. But together, exactly a year from when they
started, Jeremy's group reached their goal—and more. The
thirty-two thousand dollars they raised was enough for not

only the ultrasound machine itself, but also the training necessary to operate it. Jeremy still can't talk about it without mentioning his sister Diana and two of his best friends.

"There's no way I could have done it by myself," Jeremy said. "I would've gotten frustrated and bored or just burnt out. They really gave me the support and encouragement to keep going."

Jeremy's story is a great example of why we gain such advantage by working "along with those" who share our resolve to do hard things for the glory of God.

For an in-depth look at how teen collaboration works—and at some of its unique challenges—let's return to one of our favorite collaboration stories ever: how Kelsey got the answer to her questions about modesty.

"Could I Post Some Questions?"

In September 2006, Kelsey stumbled across TheRebelution .com and joined the forum. It wasn't long before she got involved in a discussion on modesty in the Girls Only section—and it was there that she had an idea. With hundreds of like-minded Christian teens on one website, what if they could start a discussion on modesty?

When we first received her note, all we knew was that a fifteen-year-old girl from Massachusetts wanted to get Christian guys to give their opinions on modesty. She wrote:

I think girls see girls differently than boys do. Do you think I could post some questions for the guys to answer about what they think is modest and immodest?

We wrote back to say that it sounded *possible,* as long as the questions and answers were posted anonymously and used the guys' and girls' private forums. A few days later we received an almost identical question from another girl. When we mentioned it to other girls and guys, we received enthusiastic responses.

We decided to explore the idea. Kelsey opened a thread in the girls' section of the forum and invited readers to submit questions they had for the guys. In a week we had more than 350 questions from hundreds of high-school and college-age Christian girls from around the world. They wanted to know how guys felt about everything from lip gloss to swimsuits to sheer sleeves—along with open-ended questions like, "As a guy, what's your responsibility in this area?"

Besides the forum thread, Kelsey was receiving dozens of e-mails a day. "My inbox was swamped," she said. "I was extremely surprised that *so many* other girls were curious about the same things as me."

We realized we were on to something important. Clearly it wasn't just Kelsey's question anymore. Christian girls around the world wanted to better understand how their clothing affected guys. Others wanted to honor God by the way they dressed, but weren't sure where to start. One thing was clear: they had a lot of questions.

After praying about it and talking with our parents, we decided we would attempt an online modesty survey. But how? Just the issue of how to format questions for the guys to answer was daunting. We would need a secure system that could collect and track answers. But none of us knew how to do that, and we didn't have money to hire professional help.

Enter David Boskovic, the rebelutionary tech whiz from Canada who had helped us launch our full website earlier that year. In between schoolwork, milking the cows, and running a family business with his older brother, David volunteered his time to design an extremely professional "smart" survey system. It was so good that a survey expert from New York contacted us to ask which company had built it for us. Imagine their surprise when we told them it was an eighteen-year-old—and that he did it from the ground up in less than a month.

The system would track which questions the participants had answered and allow them to return as many times as needed to complete the survey. Each question was rephrased as a statement (for example, "Bikini swimsuits are immodest") with which guys could agree or disagree on a five-point scale. Every question included a text box for the guys to further explain their responses. Many questions also included links to pop-up windows with photo illustrations and definitions.

Those were compiled by our fifteen-year-old sister, Sarah, and a team of girls from the forum. Honestly, how many teen guys know what gauchos or shrugs are?

On January 8, 2007, we opened the 148-question survey. We hoped for at least a hundred male responders. Best-case scenario, a thousand, but that didn't seem realistic.

But what did we know? In the first day, we heard from 120 guys, and within three weeks our total respondents numbered 1,700 Christian guys from forty-eight states and twenty-six countries. Together they had submitted 160,000 answers—including over 25,000 text responses.

The next task was to process the data. We wanted to release the results on Valentine's Day as a gift to all Christian girls striving to dress modestly. That date left us with just two and a half weeks to wade through 3,290 pages of data. Fortunately, David's incredible programming allowed us to automatically process our findings. That made it possible for us to focus on the text responses, selecting the top twenty to fifty for each question.

For two weeks our living room was filled with stacks of survey results and scattered with highlighters, pens, and paper clips. After several all-nighters—including several thirty-six-hour days—we released the results. By then 130 teens had volunteered to mention the survey on their blogs, send e-mail blasts, or hand out cards at their schools and churches.

Then we waited.

The first signs were *not* encouraging. About an hour after launching the results we started getting reports that the website was running really slow. "That's weird," we thought. "We're on a fast server. What is going on?"

Here's the story from Kelsey's perspective:

[That morning] when I went on to find the link to the results, the website took about five minutes to load. I thought it was very strange, and when it finally did load, people kept saying that the survey was kicking them off. In my ignorance of the Internet, I thought maybe a couple hundred people were on there.

Later, when I was instant messaging a friend, she said something about ten thousand people looking at it in the first hour. It was so many that the server had actually shut down.

I couldn't believe it! I was so excited that I was jumping around the house yelling, "Ten thousand people in the first hour!" despite the fact that I had a sore throat and a fever. My sister said she was going to whack me on the head with her cookie tray if I didn't stop screaming!

It wasn't until later that we got the full report from David: even with the server down for over an hour, the survey had received 420,000 hits in the first twelve hours.

What an amazing experience! Our team received hundreds of comments and e-mails expressing gratitude for the survey. One of the most common responses was from girls who were blown away that so many guys actually appreciated their efforts to dress modestly—and cared enough to take the survey. Our favorite response, though, was from Kelsey herself, reflecting on what had come from her sincere question and simple idea:

> I was amazed that the survey became so big. It started with my little idea and grew into a project with thousands of people involved.
>
> The survey isn't legalistic and there are no "rules" from it, but the answers allow girls to get a glimpse into the minds of guys. There is *no way* I could've done something like this on my own.
>
> I've always wanted to have an impact. Somehow I wanted to encourage Christian girls to dress more modestly, but I never dreamed I would actually have a chance to have such widespread influence.
>
> It was the first time a big dream of mine came true.

The satisfaction that comes from knowing that what we've accomplished together dwarfs anything we could've done alone is something we've seen before. We saw this truth play out beautifully with the Modesty Survey, the Alabama Supreme Court races, and our Rebelution Tour conferences.

We want to pass on a few things we've learned about collaboration that might help you when you're faced with an important task that's too big to accomplish alone.

TEN THINGS WE'VE LEARNED ABOUT TEAMS

Walk into any Barnes & Noble and you'll find entire aisles devoted almost entirely to the subject of collaboration. It's called the business section. We recommend you spend some time there. We obviously can't compete with authors who are wiser and more experienced on such a complex subject. Besides, we don't need to rewrite what is written there. We simply offer a teens'-eye view of where to start, how to avoid a few common pitfalls, and ultimately how to harness the power of collaboration to accomplish big hard things for God.

1. Start with Questions

The first thing you need to do is ask yourself some foundational questions:

- *What is God saying to me about this idea?*
- *What is the advice of my parents and others I trust?*
- *Am I the one to lead? If not, can I be a catalyst and help get things moving?*

- *What are my personal strengths and weaknesses?*
- *Which people I know can help fill the gaps where my ability or knowledge falls short?*
- *Do I care enough about this issue to not just start something big, but to see it through no matter what?*

As you saw in Kelsey's story, God *does* give guidance and help to those who are seeking Him. You might get all green lights, or you might see a lot of yellows or even reds. Make sure you ask—and listen—before you launch.

2. Walk with the Wise

Right from the beginning, look to those who are older and wiser for reliable guidance. One of our favorite verses about collaboration is Proverbs 13:20: "Whoever walks with the wise becomes wise, but the companion of fools will suffer harm." This verse reminds us that friends can be a curse or a blessing depending on whether they are wise or foolish. It also tells us that we become like our friends. You've heard the old saying, "You are what you eat." It's probably just as accurate to say, "You are who you hang out with." If we want to be wise, mature, and godly, we have to make friends with people who have those qualities.

Walking with the wise usually means spending time with those who are older, more experienced, and godlier than we are. This is one reason why we find it so important to be plugged in to our local church—the number one source we've found for wise and godly companionship.

Walking with the wise has special significance for collaboration. Proverbs 20:29 says that the glory of youth is "their strength" and that the glory of the old is their "gray hair." In ancient Israel, gray hair symbolized dignity, honor, experience, and wisdom. Teens have a lot of energy, but we don't always know what to do with it; older people often have better insight but don't always have the time or energy to see it through. The beauty of collaboration between older and younger generations is that we combine strength with wisdom—a surefire way to accomplish more for the glory of God.

3. Don't Overlook Home Field Advantage

Family is a God-designed vehicle for collaboration that most teens miss, even though we're right in the middle of it. God intended your parents to be your primary mentors, and unless you're an only child, siblings can be some of your best team members.

Look back at the stories we've covered in this chapter: Kelsey's biggest supporter and mentor was always her mom; Jeremy's main assistant was his sister Diana. We've seen this over and over in our own lives and in the stories of countless teens.

The Rebelution conferences are put on for teens by teens. The local coordinators for our Denver and Dallas events in

2007, Joanna Griffith and Marshall Sherman, were seventeen and sixteen when they started work securing facilities and assembling their local teams. We had publicity captains as young as thirteen spreading the word in their schools, local papers, and youth groups. Our facility captain in Denver, Robert Anderson—in charge of event setup and logistics—was fourteen.

Although teens have the titles and carry the responsibility, it's a whole-family affair. Joanna's parents ran countless errands and manned the book tables and checkout station. Her sister, Susanna, was the refreshments captain for the event, providing lunch and snacks for over five hundred people. Joanna's other siblings helped by running errands, carrying boxes, stuffing name tags in plastic holders, and any number of other tasks.

In our family, not only is our father one of the main speakers at the conferences, but our older brother Joel leads worship. When it comes to organization, schedules, supplies, accounting—and everything in between—our mother is a third-degree black belt. Our sister Sarah helps to coordinate volunteers, makes phone calls, sends e-mails, folds and arranges hundreds of "do hard things" T-shirts, stuffs name tags, and is our mom's right-hand girl. Our thirteen-year-old brother, Isaac, is a jack-of-all-trades. Before the events he is in charge of brochure mailings—packing, addressing, and mailing hundreds of envelopes to families around the country.

Even our seven-year-old brother, James, helps. At the Indianapolis conference in 2007, he spent hours with older volunteers, zip-tying over two thousand folding chairs into straight, even rows.

By the way, when we let younger kids work alongside us, we're doing for them what we ask of our older mentors. When they walk with us, relatively speaking, they walk with the wise. They get to be mentored in how and why to do hard things. We get energetic and enthusiastic help. Everybody wins.

We understand that not everyone has a family like ours, and we'd be exaggerating if we tried to make our family sound anything near perfect. But we hope you catch a vision for collaborating with family—if not with the family you have now, then with other families in your community and with the family you'll have someday.

4. Use Technology to Grow Your Team

One of the greatest benefits of modern technology is that it lets us connect with like-minded people regardless of location. Many of our best friends are people we know primarily online, and yet we've been able to work together on some exciting projects.

The Modesty Survey is one fine example. The Alabama campaigns are another. For one candidate's website design, we used a company that is the co-enterprise of Jake Smith and another rebelutionary Alex King. Alex lives in Maine and Jake in Oklahoma. They've still never met, but they delivered top-notch service.

These same guys, along with several other online friends, also headed up an online magazine, podcast, and blog network for Christian teens called Regenerate Our Culture. It ran for almost two years and brought together teen writers, editors, and radio hosts from around the world. Hardly any of them ever met in person.

In fact, one of the most common responses we've received since launching TheRebelution.com is from young people who thought they were all alone in their convictions about the teen years. They express how grateful and relieved they are to finally find a community of like-minded teens—and it's all online. So take advantage of technology.

5. Treasure Constructive Criticism

From early on in the development of the Modesty Survey, we asked for and received counsel from family and friends. Modesty is a sensitive topic, and we knew that we needed help framing the questions. We also knew that the survey results could easily come across as a list of rules or as a bunch of guys telling girls how to dress. We didn't want that. Thankfully we were able to receive high-quality input as we developed the survey, which helped us provide biblical teaching on modesty in the weeks leading up to its release. Of course, getting corrective input doesn't always feel good at the time. It would have been easy to react defensively to the criticism. But without it, we could've ended up doing more harm than good.

6. Credit Is Free if You Give It Away

One of the common dangers we've come across is that pride (for example, looking for credit or taking offense when we feel overlooked) often sabotages team efforts. What to do? We recommend dealing quickly and respectfully with hurt feelings. We also recommend establishing a team code that says, "Credit is free around here, and *we give it away*." That helps individuals focus on the needs and accomplishments of others and of the group as a whole and makes for a much happier, healthier, and more effective team.

Any one of us involved in the Modesty Survey could've made a wreck of the project if we had been seeking all the credit. Kelsey could have demanded a bigger role in everything—it was *her* idea. We could have tried to take all of the glory—it was *our* website. And David could have done the same thing (plus charge a lot of money we didn't have)—it was *his* survey system, and none of it would've been possible without him. But thankfully none of that happened. Instead we focused on accomplishing something we believed in, and thousands have been blessed as a result.

7. Other People Are Sinners Too

Probably the hardest thing about working with other people is that you actually have to work *with* them. Know what we mean? Even good, solid, sincere Christians are sinful and imperfect (that is, difficult if not impossible at times). And pressure, weariness, and frustration often bring out the worst in people. That's why big hard things require patience, humility, and a nearly endless supply of forgiveness.

One of the reasons we love stories like Kelsey's and Jeremy's is that they're all about big hard things being accomplished by a group of ordinary teens. One of the things our dad likes to say about the church is that it "runs on regular." The same is true about the Rebelution, and it's certainly true about accomplishing big hard things—it doesn't take superheroes or saints. It just takes a small handful of like-minded people willing to do hard things together and extend a lot of grace along the way.

8. Expect a Nightmare or Two

Over the course of putting together the survey—and working on the campaigns in Alabama—we ran into countless miscommunications, disagreements, and silly mistakes. At times the unbelievable, impossible, and disastrous happened—all at the same time.

For example, in the process of organizing the successful

distribution of over 120,000 campaign newspapers at the Talladega Superspeedway Aaron's 499—an enormous event with hundreds of thousands of people in a single weekend—we ran into more than our share of what felt like minor catastrophes.

First, the fifty college students driving in from four states away forgot to factor in the time difference and arrived an hour before we were ready for them. We didn't have sign-in sheets to check them in, and pizza hadn't been delivered yet. It was a bad start.

Then we discovered a major miscommunication. The students' professor had told them they'd be campaigning for the governor's race—not the supreme court races. When they found out, they were disappointed, and some were upset. They felt like they had been tricked, and a few of them wanted to leave right then and there.

At this point, only three campaign members were at the campground: Alex, Brett, and another seventeen-year-old named Jonathan Monplaisir. We wanted to crawl into a hole and die. Then the college students found out how old we were—and that we were in charge—and it seemed like things couldn't get any worse. Thankfully they didn't.

We made a lot of phone calls and were able to get the candidates there quickly to give the students a pep talk. We called the professor and obtained a statement from him admitting that the mistake was his and that he firmly believed that helping our candidates was just as important as helping the governor's race.

Over the course of that evening, we were able to pull things back together, get pizza to the hungry students, assemble over one thousand campaign signs, load tens of thousands of newspapers into the vehicles, and get everyone into bed. Compared to those first few hours, the next two days went like clockwork.

Nightmares happen. But we shouldn't be surprised. The Bible warns us that when we actively pursue Christ's mission, we'll face obstacles. So our best response is to be forewarned—and not to panic when it happens. Actually, we've found that nightmares give your prayer life a real boost—and teach you a whole lot at warp speed. Protect yourself and your team from being discouraged by looking for God's hand in every situation.

9. Don't Give Up

Successful collaboration almost always requires a lot of people working together over a long period of time. So teamwork requires perseverance.

It would have been easy for Kelsey to give up on her big idea long before it came about. She didn't know anyone else who could (or would) help her. Even on our forums, the initial response to her idea of asking guys questions about modesty was less than enthusiastic. Other girls pointed out how awkward a public discussion on the topic would be. She almost gave up altogether, but her mom encouraged her to keep going and to ask us directly. "It took some convincing," she says, "but I'm so glad I didn't give up."

10. Success Happens (in More Ways than One)

We've found that collaboration is not just *how* we accomplish big hard things; it often turns into a big hard thing itself. That means we should measure our success not just by the goal we're shooting for, but also by how well we work together to get there. Look inside your team effort for small but important victories—personal firsts, spiritual breakthroughs, tough to-do lists completed, lessons learned, total disasters turned into qualified successes. They're all successes of different kinds, and they're all important.

Our two major collaborative efforts—the Alabama campaigns and the Modesty Survey—had very different final results. The Modesty Survey turned out better than we'd ever imagined. We lost the elections. But in a way, both were successful because the young people involved grew stronger in the process. They made real accomplishments, gained valuable experience, impacted others for good, and learned lessons about teamwork and big hard things that they'll be able to hold on to forever.

Tackling Big Hard Things

The most exciting thing about stepping up to the challenge of big hard things is that when God calls on you, He will bring the help you need to get the job done. So don't be afraid of tackling big goals with others. Your first big hard thing might not be raising thirty-two thousand dollars, coordinating a grass-roots campaign, or launching an online survey. But just like with any hard thing, the big hard things you can accomplish will get bigger as you get stronger.

We hope you've seen that big projects don't have to wait until later. Together we can accomplish great things for God, starting today. We love the way Kelsey put it:

> At the time, nothing seemed at all strange, but when I look back on it now, it totally blows me away. We were all eighteen or younger. I was only fifteen. It makes me wonder, what *more* is possible when teens work together? There were about five main people working on the Modesty Survey. Imagine what we could do with a team of one hundred people!

What could *you* do with three people, or ten, or a hundred? Pray and plan. Then go for it.

SMALL HARD THINGS

How to do hard things that don't pay off immediately

Joanna hung up the phone in shock. She had been counting down the days until the trip to Romania for months. Now her father had called to say the trip had been canceled.

"I was heartbroken," Joanna told us later. "I felt as if I'd been pushed underwater without being able to catch a breath."

That summer, instead of an exciting trip to Romania to share the gospel, Joanna found herself stuck at home in

Tennessee. With her mother experiencing some serious health problems, and as the oldest child at home, Joanna was the one to head up meals, sort laundry, care for younger siblings, and clean.

It wasn't exactly the summer she had planned. "It was *hard*," Joanna said. "One of the hardest times of my life."

Have you ever felt like Joanna? Ready and motivated to tackle something big and exciting but stuck against your will in a seemingly endless round of chores?

How do we reconcile the fact that there's a big world out there to impact for God with the fact that we're stuck at home matching socks in yet another load of laundry? What are rebelutionaries to make of all the small, seemingly insignificant things that take up so much time and energy? How do things like doing the dishes and writing lab reports for biology fit into "do hard things"?

Rebelutionaries have to think straight about this problem or we'll get ambushed on our way to doing big hard things for God. And what's more, we'll miss out on the genuine significance and hidden benefits of what we like to call "small hard things."

Mending Nets and Gutting Fish

In Rudyard Kipling's classic novel *Captains Courageous*, fifteen-year-old Harvey Cheyne, the son of a wealthy railroad tycoon, is washed overboard from a transatlantic steamship and rescued by fishermen.

Cold, wet, and forgotten for the first time in his spoiled existence, Harvey at first tries to convince the fishermen of his parents' great wealth. He wants them to abandon their fishing season and take him ashore, where he promises his father will reward them generously. But his pleas don't work. In the end he is forced to earn his keep mending nets and gutting fish.

At first Harvey can't believe his bad luck. The backbreaking work, the long hours, the stench, and the cold and wet disgust and overwhelm him. But over time, Harvey mysteriously changes. His body toughens. He learns to use his hands and his head to perform the tasks and weather the trials of fishing on the open sea. He begins to actually enjoy the hardships and to admire the strength and intelligence of his new companions.

When the boat finally returns to port, Harvey wires his parents, who rush to the small town. Amazed, they find a transformed son. Their lazy, demanding boy has become an industrious, serious, and considerate young man. No longer needing or wanting his mother's constant doting, Harvey is ready to start a successful career in his father's shipping lines.

Maybe you feel forgotten and alone, grinding away at pointless routines that seem guaranteed to lead you nowhere. You feel like you have incredible potential, but it's all going to waste.

The truth is that your life (both now and later) will require you to invest a lot of time and energy in things that aren't big and that don't seem to make much of an impact. Some days they don't even make sense. Sometimes the smallest things can be the hardest things of all.

But in this chapter we'll show you the big role that doing those small hard things can play for all of us—not just now but for the rest of our lives. We think you'll learn what Harvey did: not only is it necessary to do small hard things, but they deliver incredible dividends in the life and future of every rebelutionary.

WHY SMALL GETS SO HARD

During our legal internship, we were surprised to find that the hardest things for us weren't the projects we were given at the court. Sure, those things were difficult, but they were also usually exciting and important. The hardest things for us were the small things like keeping our room clean, going to bed on time, reading our Bible each morning, and staying in touch with our family.

You've probably experienced the same thing in your own life. For you it could be things like reading your Bible and praying. Maybe it's doing family chores when (and how) your mom wants you to. Maybe it's getting up on time, exercising regularly, or saying no to certain distractions or temptations.

For us it has often been all of those things and more. What-ever they are for you, they're not big things, but they're hard.

Small things most often occur behind the closed doors of our homes, schools, or churches. They are rarely new or excit-ing, and they are often repetitive—even tedious. Small things happen on the level at which we normally live our lives. In fact, in the most basic sense they *are* our lives—the "stuff" that makes up everyday living. You won't make it in the head-lines for any of them ("Local Boy Cleans Bedroom and Does Homework!") or wake up looking forward to them ("Oh boy! Today I get to obey my mom cheerfully!").

We tried to figure out exactly why small hard things are so difficult. See if you agree with our top five reasons:

1. *They don't usually go away after you do them.* "My bedroom doesn't stay clean. The dishes don't stay washed. Teeth don't stay brushed. There's always another test for school and another temptation to say no to. Over and over. Does it ever stop?"

2. *They don't seem very important.* "Spending time with my little brother isn't as important as raising money for orphans in Africa or volunteering for a political campaign. I'm supposed to do big things for God. This is a distraction."

3. *They don't seem to make any difference.* "In five years will it really matter whether I cleaned my room today? Or whether I drove the speed limit to work?

Or whether I read my Bible this morning? How do I benefit from doing these things?"

4. *They don't seem very glamorous.* "I don't get any props for holding my temper with my dad. No one even knows. And now I'm cleaning the bathroom. It's a gross and thankless job. Yuck. This is not what I signed up for."

5. *No one is watching.* "Everyone's impressed because she's running a charity for cancer patients. No one knows or cares that I'm taking care of Grandma and studying for my SATs."

Unfortunately, we tend to respond to these small hard things in not-so-rebelutionary ways. So besides naming five reasons small things are hard, we also came up with *five ways we fail to do small hard things.* See if you can recognize yourself in any of the following:

1. *Procrastination.* "Sure, I'll take care of that—eventually. In just a minute. Right after I... Oh, look. It's time for bed."

2. *Inconsistency.* "Yeah, I read my Bible. In fact I just read it this morning. Of course I didn't do it yesterday or the day before, but I did last Tuesday...I think."

3. *Compromise.* "I'll do it just this once. One time can't hurt, right? Maybe just one more time. Then I'll stop for good. Oh... Just one more time."

4. *Begrudging.* "Okay, I'll do it if I have to! Just don't expect me to do it with a decent attitude."

5. *Cheating.* "Look, I cleaned my room really well. At least if you don't look in the closet, or under the bed, or in my dresser, or in my laundry hamper."

Small things often *seem* routine, insignificant, and pointless. But are they?

We don't think so. The evidence of wisdom, the Bible, history, and the experiences of people like Joanna show otherwise.

The truth is that huge gifts are often hiding in those small packages.

THE PLAN BEHIND THE PAIN

"God had a plan," Joanna says, reflecting on her canceled trip to Romania and the summer spent taking care of her family. "And it was *much* better than mine. Had this never happened, I wouldn't have learned how to cook better, help my younger siblings, or take care of things around the house. I can honestly say that I'm thankful for this trial, even though it was extremely hard."

Like Harvey in *Captains Courageous,* Joanna learned that small things equip you for big things in the future. Habits like working hard, maintaining a positive attitude, living with self-discipline and integrity, and serving others bring benefits

to our lives now *and* pay enormous dividends in the future—
if we do them faithfully.

Take a careful look at the drudgery you're stuck in today.
If it's making an effort to be kind to a sibling, you're accomplishing at least two things: shaping your future relationship
with that brother or sister and training yourself for how you
will relate to your future spouse and co-workers. If you're slogging through chemistry today, you're affecting your academic
future while also exercising and strengthening your brain to
figure out complex situations later in life.

Doing hard things is how we exercise our bodies, our
minds, and our faith. Small hard things are the individual repetitions—like a single push-up. They are seemingly insignificant by themselves but guaranteed to get results over time.

As you might expect, God cares a great deal about small
things, and the Bible has a lot to say about them. In the gospel
of Matthew, Jesus shares the Parable of the Talents. In this
story, a nobleman gives each of his servants a certain amount
of money (called "talents") before leaving on a journey. When
he returns, two of the servants report that they put his money
to work and doubled what he'd given them. The master commends each of these servants, saying, "You have been faithful
over a little; I will set you over much" (25:21). The gospel of
Luke tells us that the "much" he was talking about was entire
cities. You couldn't ask for a better promotion than that.

But the third servant—the one who did nothing at all with what he had been given—got rebuked. "You wicked and slothful servant!" his master said, and he had the lazy man thrown out into the street (Matthew 25:26). Even what he had was lost.

Another picture of small things in the Bible is in Galatians 6:7, where Paul writes, "Do not be deceived: God is not mocked, for whatever one sows, that will he also reap." Every action, no matter how small, is defining our future harvest. Small seeds can make big weeds, but they can also produce beautiful flowers or feed a nation.

But that's where lazy servants (and many of us) get tripped up. We enjoy the harvest, but we don't enjoy sowing and cultivating good seed. We enjoy being fit and strong, but we don't enjoy exercise. We all want to do big and important things, but we tend to discount the equally important small things that get us there.

That's where the "do hard things" mentality comes in. It reminds us that sometimes the smallest things can be the hardest things and that the purpose of effort is to gain strength. Being faithful in the smallest things is the way to gain, maintain, and demonstrate the strength needed to accomplish something great.

One of the best examples of this that we've found is the Vikings. And no, we're not talking about the football team.

A Lesson from the Vikings

The Vikings were fierce pirates and warriors who terrorized northern Europe nearly a thousand years ago. They looted and burned pretty much every European country that had the misfortune to border the Atlantic Ocean. Europeans were so frightened of the Viking menace that churches often offered a special prayer: "God, deliver us from the fury of the Northmen."

Most historians attribute the Vikings' devastating effectiveness to their warships, which were light enough to be dragged up onto the beach. That allowed the raiders to make lightning-fast strikes, then retreat quickly to the safety of the sea.

However, another contributing factor holds great significance for rebelutionaries: the Vikings rowed themselves to battle. Most other sea powers at that time used slaves or professional rowers to propel their warships, but the Vikings took full responsibility for that repetitive and strenuous activity. That tells us one very important thing about them: they were seriously ripped.

No wonder an entire continent lived in dread of them. By sheer muscle power, they routinely moved twenty-ton boats across miles of ocean. When they got out of their boats and started swinging their battle-axes, it didn't matter if you carried a shield or barricaded your door. You stood little chance.

The Vikings' incredible upper-body strength made them nearly undefeatable.

We can all learn a lesson about small hard things from the Vikings. *If* we're willing to strive for excellence, even in the boring, repetitive tasks and responsibilities that others delegate or neglect, we *will* reap the powerful benefits that others miss.

Embracing small hard things can make a radical difference.

CHECK, CHECK, CHECK!

"I've always been a procrastinator," Katie, a high-school junior, admitted in a letter. "I thought I always *would be* a procrastinator. I thought that despite all my hopes and dreams I'd still fail." Katie told us she avoided anything she didn't want to do for as long as possible and routinely turned in school assignments late. "The dictionary defines a procrastinator as someone who 'puts off intentionally and habitually the doing of something that should be done.' That would be me," she confessed.

For Katie, the turnaround moment came when she got an F in Algebra 2. That really woke her up. Suddenly she could see herself flipping burgers at a fast-food joint *for a career.* That's when she decided to tackle her own very hard thing: procrastination.

"This time, I vowed, would be different. I chose my classes carefully. I got my priorities straight. I quit the volleyball team. I set my alarm clock. I made a schedule and stuck to it like glue. I didn't want to give myself the chance to turn back."

Several months after taking aim at her procrastination problem, Katie's life has changed dramatically. Here's how she describes her life now:

I'm not behind in anything. In fact, I'm ahead of schedule in a couple things. I just got an A on a history test last week. I had time to accept a regular baby-sitting job and participate in some extracurricular activities like debate and speech. I actually have time to sit down and write this story.

Overcoming my procrastination is the hardest thing I've ever had to do. That might seem trivial to you, but to me it is a thing of beauty. I am not useless. I still have a chance to pursue my dreams. Of course, I have to stay committed, but now that I know it's possible, I am not about to go back to the way things were.

My assignment book has become my most priceless piece of work with all its beautiful markings: check, check, check!

What small hard things have popped into your mind as you've read the stories of Joanna, Harvey, Katie, and the

Vikings? If you're like us, there will always be certain tasks or responsibilities you want to overlook. We constantly have to remind ourselves that it really is of utmost importance to keep an eye on those areas where we tend to let things slide. Here are a couple of questions to help you do the same:

- Think of a regular or daily task you hate that takes less than five minutes a day. How do you most often deal with it? Procrastination? Inconsistency? Irritation? How might you benefit from a shift in attitude and a renewed commitment to this small thing?

- Do you have a big goal for your life that you can't achieve without a commitment to small hard things? Write down your big goal. Then write out the small hard things that will help you achieve it—and how faithfully doing those small hard things now will help you achieve your dream later.

Remember, as you commit today to excellence, doing the small hard things God has given you, He will give you strength. Over time the tasks *will* get easier, and the benefits of doing them will become more and more obvious.

"HERE LIVED A GREAT STREET SWEEPER"

Now for a hard question: can we assign meaning to the simplest and humblest of acts? It's not extremely difficult to recognize that the faithful practice of doing small hard things should be valued as vital preparation for future achievements, but are they significant in and of themselves?

Yes. Every job we do with sincere effort and the right attitude brings pleasure to God. In Colossians 3:23, Paul wrote, "*Whatever you do,* work at it with all your heart, as working for the Lord, not for men" (NIV). And in 1 Corinthians 10:31, he says it again: "*Whatever you do,* do all to the glory of God."

We love the way Martin Luther King Jr. addressed this issue for those in all walks of life:

> If it falls your lot to be a street sweeper, sweep streets
> like Michelangelo painted pictures, sweep streets like
> Beethoven composed music.... Sweep streets like Shake-
> speare wrote poetry. Sweep streets so well that all the
> hosts of heaven and earth will have to pause and say:
> Here lived a great street sweeper who swept his job well.

Like the street sweeper, your actions at home, at school, at church, and elsewhere in your community can bring honor and glory to God if you are willing to throw yourself into them 100 percent just because they're things *He* has given you to do.

Take up your Viking challenge today to do small hard things. The fact that you face those unwanted tasks is not a mistake; it's an opportunity. That's why we encourage you to put your full weight into every stroke of the oar.

And because God is good, by doing what He has put before you with all your heart, regardless of whether it appears significant or not, you will find yourself benefited and strengthened, ready for the next big thing.

TAKING A STAND

How to do hard things that go against the crowd

E va lives in a rural part of Germany where almost every-one is "Christian," yet few are serious about following Christ. The consensus in her village, she told us in an e-mail, is that religion won't hurt you and it just might be helpful in rough times. So when Eva, at sixteen, decided to *really* live for God, she immediately found herself at odds with the cul-ture—particularly the youth culture in her region, which revolves around weekend parties where students forget school and drink a lot of alcohol.

In Eva's world, these parties aren't considered add-ons to your social life—they *are* your social life. Even the parents in her village accept them as normal. Nearly every conversation at school during the week is tied back to the parties. It's always, "Did you see that guy with Melanie?" or, "Were you there when Daniel started dancing with the DJ?" As soon as the gossip from last week's party fades, planning for the next one begins. Life is lived from one weekend to the next, and to be part of the in crowd, you have to be there.

Everyone expects Eva to attend, but she's a Christian now. Should she choose to stay home even if it makes her a social outcast? Maybe she could just go and stand in the corner? She wouldn't want people to think Christians can't have any fun, would she?

Have you ever had to make a decision like Eva's? Maybe it was whether to go along with the group to watch a certain movie. Maybe it was not buying a certain outfit because it drew attention in the wrong way. Or maybe your teacher asked you to share your opinion in a class discussion on ethics. Suddenly a dozen pairs of eyes are turned on you. Your heart begins pounding faster and louder. Your cheeks burn red. This is your chance to stand up for what you believe, but you're afraid. What will people think? What if you say something wrong? Why is this so difficult?

Sometimes we do stand up for what we believe. We tell someone it's wrong to use God's name as a cuss word, or we ask our unbelieving friends what they think happens after they die. But more often than not, it seems we just sink deeper into our chair, focus intently on our textbook, change the subject, leave the room, or just tell our conscience to take a hike. *Our convictions are a private matter,* we rationalize (that is, rational lies). *It's important not to make waves or come across as if we're better than somebody else.*

In this chapter we focus on the fifth and final kind of rebelutionary hard thing—taking a stand, even when it's unpopular. This is one of the hardest things for teens (or anyone, really) to do. It goes against our natural desire to fit in, to be liked, to make friends. There's nothing quite like it for putting our convictions to the test. We'll look honestly at some of the costs of that decision—you could lose friends and popularity, you could lose opportunities, and in some countries you could even lose your life.

But we'll also look at some of the genuine blessings that can come as a result of standing up for what's right. It all boils down to a principle at the heart of Christian character: we have to care more about pleasing God than we care about pleasing man. As Eva is discovering, a decision like that changes almost everything about the way you live.

It can even change the course of history.

WHAT DEFINES YOU?

All of Eva's turmoil and indecision faded away when she came across the words Jesus prayed for His disciples—and for everyone who will believe throughout the ages:

> I gave them your word; the godless world hated them
> because of it, *because they didn't join the world's ways,*
> just as I didn't join the world's ways. I'm not asking
> that you take them out of the world but that you
> guard them from the Evil One. *They are no more*
> *defined by the world than I am defined by the world.*
> (John 17:14–16, MSG)

From that point onward, Eva knew she couldn't go on living like her peers. She was an ambassador—belonging to the kingdom of God and not to Germany or its youth culture. She lived in a world of parties, but she didn't have to be part of that anymore. And if the world hated her for her choice, so be it. Her mission wasn't to fit in. It was to be faithful.

It reminds us of a scene from the Rodgers and Hammerstein musical *Oklahoma!* in which the characters are performing a eulogy for that "mean ugly feller" Jud Fry. They solemnly intone:

Jud was the most misunderstood man in the territory.
People used to think that he was a mean ugly feller,
and they called him a dirty skunk and an ornery pig
stealer.

But the folks that really knowed him, knowed...
that Jud Fry loved his feller man....

He loved the birds of the forest and the beasts
of the field. He loved the mice and the vermin in
the barn, and he treated the rats like equals, which
was right. Oh, and he loved the little children.
He loved everybody and everything in the whole
world! Only he never let on, so nobody ever
knowed it.

And even though this is supposed to be a funny scene, we
need to ask ourselves if the same kind of thing couldn't be
said at our own funerals. What if Curly were performing *your*
eulogy? Would it go something like this?

Joe Teenager was the most misunderstood young man
in this here country. People used to think all he cared
about was having fun and goofing off. They called
him a rebellious teenager and a foolish kid! But the
folks that really know'd him, know'd that beneath the
laptop, the iPod, the television, the Xbox 360, his girl-
friends, his bad attitude toward his parents, his self-

centeredness, and his laziness, there beat a heart for God as big as all outdoors.

Joe Teenager loved God and his family. He knew that his teen years were his season of strict training, which was right. And he wanted to impact the world for Christ. He wanted to stand up for what was right in front of the whole world. Only he never let on, so nobody ever know'd it.

Eva realized, as we also must, that a changed heart will result in a changed life—that true saving faith in Jesus Christ will show in our actions. The apostle James wrote in James 2:18, "But someone will say, 'You have faith and I have works.' Show me your faith apart from your works, and I will show you my faith by my works." Please understand that we are saved by faith alone, but true saving faith doesn't stay alone.

This is not a call to parade our religiosity around, but it does mean that a true Christian faith will permeate our lives. It means that whether you watch a certain movie or laugh at a certain joke tells you and others something about the state of your heart.

For Eva, it meant that just going along with the crowd wasn't an option. "If being a Christian doesn't change the way I act on the outside," she reasoned, "then how can I say that there was any real change on the inside?"

Doing What's Right, Even When It Hurts

She knew she had made the right decision, but Eva still had to face the consequences of taking a stand. Her friends and classmates immediately wondered why she wasn't attending the parties. Even some of the adults in the village couldn't understand.

At school Eva was suddenly left out of all the gossip and conversation. Because she quit going to the weekend parties, her classmates started to consider her a boring outsider—a label that was very hard for Eva to take.

"I have to admit that there were times when I just wanted to fit back in," she says. "It was so hard sometimes not to be part of the crowd, not to belong to the cool group, not to have a clique of cool friends."

Eva's stand meant rejection and being misunderstood by her peers. But in other parts of the world, the consequences are even more severe. In India, two teens were surrounded and beaten for distributing Bible tracts. In China, a sixteen-year-old girl was shot in the head for refusing to spit on the Bible. Christians all over the world are persecuted, tortured, and killed for their faith.

Fortunately Eva knew what she was getting into. She had already read the Bible passages that warn that some might hate us because we don't join in the world's ways. She knew she wasn't called to follow Jesus only when she'd get pats on the back for it; she was called to follow Him even when it hurt. And if she wasn't willing to follow Him when it hurt, she wasn't really following Him at all.

Ultimately that's exactly what it means for us to take a stand: doing what's right—even when it costs us something.

We knew we were taking a stand when we posted the Modesty Survey, but we were still taken aback by the opposition it stirred up. While thousands of girls appreciated the survey as a helpful resource, hundreds of others viewed it as a list of rules or felt that we were blaming women for men's problems. Feminist websites wrote scathing articles calling us "sexually repressed fundamentalists" and sent hundreds of their readers to our site to leave angry comments. Many of these visitors never took the time to actually study the survey results for themselves but jumped to the conclusion that we hate women and want to see them dressed in burlap sacks. For every handful of thankful e-mails, we would receive at least one obscenity-laced message telling us exactly what we deserved for our "judgmental attitude." Even Kelsey had a friend rant to her about the survey, not realizing that she was one of its creators.

If we hadn't known we would face opposition for taking a stand, we all could've been overwhelmed and discouraged. But in a culture that glorifies impurity, it's not surprising that some feel threatened by a group of teens that wants to be pure.

When we make decisions to obey God—even when it costs us something—and to live out our faith in our day-to-day life, it will be hard, but it will be good. And it will be good because God loves to bless us when we are faithful to stand for Him.

WE'LL ALWAYS BE GLAD WE DID

Remember the Old Testament story of Joseph getting sold into slavery by his jealous older brothers? Years later, when a famine has swept the land and the brothers are begging for food, they meet up again with Joseph, who has risen to become a ruler of Egypt—and the keeper of the food store-houses. When they realize who Joseph is, the brothers fear for their lives, but Joseph reassures them with a memorable insight that any rebelutionary who's taken a few hits will appreciate. Joseph tells his brothers, "You intended to harm me, but God intended it for good to accomplish what is now being done, the saving of many lives" (Genesis 50:20, NIV).

When we take a stand for God, we'll often suffer per-secution of different kinds. But God *is* at work. Good is being accomplished in many lives—and so often *we* are the beneficiaries.

Eva's decision to forgo the weekend parties provided her with many unexpected benefits, including the opportunity to grow closer to her family. "I did lots of things with my brother and sisters," Eva shares, laughing. "And we had lots of fun together."

Not only that, but over time the school situation got better as well. "My classmates began to respect me," Eva told us. "They couldn't always understand my behavior, but they tolerated it." And even though she was still sometimes branded an outsider at school, Eva did get to know some really nice girls. "We started driving to school together, and we studied for our exams," she says. "Doing such normal things helped them realize that I wasn't a strange kid!"

Most important, Eva feels that God protected her from a lot of heartache and pain. "I was kept safe and pure for Him," she explains. "He gave me strength and wisdom and didn't let me become lonely." What Eva learned is that the right thing, though hard, really is the smartest—and in many ways the easier—thing. *Easier?* you ask.

Consider: Ten years from now, if you were to ask Eva's partying classmates what they thought was harder—staying home from all the parties for two years of high school or dealing with the consequences of alcohol and drug addiction, broken relationships, unwanted pregnancies, and sexually transmitted diseases—they'd probably say that Eva made the "easier" choice. And they'd be right.

Or ask Jordan, a fifteen-year-old attending high school in Sacramento, California. He went along with a large group of other teens to watch the football movie *Invincible* only to find out that the other kids were really planning to sneak into the

R-rated movie *Beerfest.* He watched as his best friend, Josh, purchased their two tickets to *Invincible,* but he could tell that Josh was thinking of sneaking into *Beerfest* too.

"I'd be lying if I said that I didn't wrestle with the decision in my mind," admits Jordan. "But then I said, *No, I'm not going there. God, I'm going to obey You.*" He leaned over and told Josh, "We don't need to see that movie, man. Let's just go see *Invincible* and do the right thing. I'm going to see *Invincible.* I'm asking you to come with me. It's your choice." That encouragement ended up being all Josh needed, and the two of them went and enjoyed *Invincible* by themselves.

The next Monday the rest of their group got busted for going to see *Beerfest,* and Jordan and Josh were the only ones who didn't get in trouble. "It was a hard choice at the time," Jordan told us, "but the long-term results really paid off, not just at school but also having a spiritual victory to remind Satan of next time."

For Jordan, Josh, and Eva, doing the hard thing of taking a stand really ended up being the easier choice in the end. And even though doing the right thing won't always result in an obvious benefit for us in this life, it *will* in the life to come.

It's like the quote by Jim Elliot, whose life was cut short tragically when he and four friends were killed bringing the gospel to the Auca people in Ecuador: "He is no fool who gives up what he cannot keep to gain that which he cannot lose."

When we understand that, doing the hard thing of taking

a stand will always be the easiest choice. Through every stand, God will strengthen our convictions and our faith—and we'll be prepared for even bigger challenges in the future.

KNOWING WHEN AND HOW TO STAND

But before you start throwing your body in front of any bull-dozers, let's think more carefully about *when* we should take a stand as well as *how* we should go about it. The fact is that we can make a big deal about something that isn't really that important. We need wisdom to understand how to properly evaluate each situation so that we can stand at the right time, for the right thing, and for the right reasons.

With that in mind, here are six principles we suggest to guide rebelutionaries in choosing to take a stand:

1. Start with the Bible.
2. Examine yourself.
3. Listen to your conscience.
4. Seek godly counsel.
5. Be humble, loving, and bold.
6. Be part of the solution.

Start with the Bible

What does God's Word say on this topic? Even if the activity isn't directly forbidden, is it in line with scriptural principles in general? Eva found the answer to her questions by reading

John 17:14–16. She wasn't supposed to be defined by this world; she was to be defined by Christ. Being a regular student of God's Word is the best way to ensure that you know when and how to stand.

Also, as you get started, don't get all caught up with obscure issues like whether it's unbiblical for someone to dye their hair purple (hint: it's not). Just because something is new, odd, or distasteful to some doesn't necessarily mean it's unbiblical. Scripture holds more than enough clear commands (for example, "Children, obey your parents"). Always start with what God's Word is clear about.

Examine Yourself

Don't get caught up trying to get a speck out of someone else's eye and ignore the log sticking out of your own (see Matthew 7:3–5). Challenging cultural norms starts with you and with the commands from God you already know but may be used to ignoring. This doesn't mean you have to be perfect before you can instruct anyone else, but it does mean you must be fighting the fight yourself. People who aren't even trying to practice what they preach are called hypocrites. Don't be a hypocrite.

Listen to Your Conscience

Our conscience is our God-given sense of what is right and what is wrong, and as we read and apply His Word, it becomes more finely tuned. If you find yourself thinking that it might be time to take a stand, it's probably because your conscience is flashing the warning lights. Listen up. In 1 Timothy 4:2, the apostle Paul talks about people whose consciences are "seared" by constant ignoring. Society expects young people to enjoy doing stuff they know is wrong, but they're not counting the cost. If you can't do something with a clear conscience, even if other people can, you shouldn't be doing it (see Romans 14:23).

A Navajo Indian tradition says that your conscience is like a small triangle inside your heart. When you know something is wrong, it turns and pricks the flesh of your heart with one of its corners. But when you harden your heart and ignore your conscience, it keeps turning, wearing down its corners in the effort to get your attention. Eventually the triangle gets so worn down that it becomes smooth and circular, spinning around and around in your heart but to no use. You can't even feel it anymore.

It's not just our own consciences we're supposed to watch out for. The apostle Paul warns against doing things that you know could encourage a brother or sister in Christ to violate his or her own conscience (see 1 Corinthians 8). Sometimes we have to take a stand for the sake of someone else—like when the group wants to watch a movie you know your friend's parents don't want him to see.

Seek Godly Counsel

Unless you simply don't have time to ask for advice (for example, when you have to make a fast decision), you should always seek the opinion of those who are more godly and experienced than you. Tell them what you think God's Word says about the topic, as well as what your own conscience tells you; then ask them what they would do in your position.

Be Humble, Loving, and Bold

The attitude with which you take a stand says just as much as the stand itself. People who always seem to be looking for a fight, who treat those who disagree with them with contempt, or who take a stand out of anger or retaliation cause more harm than good.

We can (and must) stand boldly—even forcefully if the situation requires it—but our standing should always be done with loving humility. We must hate the sin, not the sinner. Apart from God's grace, not one of us is saved or sanctified.

Take a look at this e-mail from a guy who observed our response to the angry comments about the Modesty Survey. His e-mail was a response not to the content of our stand, which he disagreed with, but to the demeanor with which we carried it out. In the end, our attitude was a testimony to the truth of what we were saying:

I just wanted to say that I really appreciate the way you guys have been handling the recent influx of dissenting comments. Strangely enough, I'm a reader of both The Rebelution [blog] and the website from which I suspect most of those commenters hail.

I'm glad that [you are treating them] civilly and that their comments aren't being deleted. The contrast between the treatment they're receiving here and the treatment most rebelutionaries would receive over there is, I'm afraid, dramatic.

The fact that you guys are keeping it kind is a strong testament to Christian values. Though I'm a liberal, pro-choice, anti-war, mostly atheistic kind of guy, I'm appalled at the nastiness expressed in most of their comments. I really appreciate that you guys work with such civility and conviction for what you believe.

Be Part of the Solution

Don't get a reputation for always being *against* everything: be *for* something. Try not to point out problems without providing solutions. Make it your goal to show people a better way—God's way—not just that their current direction is wrong.

Jessica Leonard (fifteen), Megan Dutill (sixteen), and Jo-anna Suich (seventeen) were tired of how superficial most teen girl magazines were—even the Christian ones. But instead of just cursing the darkness, these girls chose to light a candle, launching their own publication for Christian girls called *Bloom!* (bloom-blog.blogspot.com). Their example is one each of us should follow.

Our ultimate goal is not just that those around us would stop joining the world's ways but that they would learn to love and embrace God's way. We can accomplish this by being passionate ambassadors, eager to proclaim the goodness of God and stand for Him before the watching world.

And as rebelutionaries, our stand for what is good and right today will have an even bigger impact than we may realize.

If You Want to Stand, Stand Now

The film *Amazing Grace* tells the inspiring story of William Wilberforce's long fight to end the slave trade in the British Empire, but our first glimpse of the man is not standing in the halls of Parliament, inspecting a rotting slave ship, or meeting with the colorful members of the famous Clapham Sect. Instead, director Michael Apted introduces Wilberforce to us as a man willing to stop his carriage in the pouring rain and slog through the mud in order to stop some men from beating their weary horse. "If you let it rest for a bit, it should get up on its own," Wilberforce informs them, now sopping wet himself. Apted's point is clear. This man stands up for the oppressed wherever and whenever he finds them—not just in the House of Lords and not just when the world is watching.

It wasn't Martin Luther's first stand when he nailed his *Ninety-Five Theses* to the door of the Castle Church in Wittenberg. He had learned to trust God with his life long before he was summoned before the Holy Roman Emperor and given the choice to either recant or be branded a heretic and thrown outside the protection of the law. There, before the most powerful men of his day, he said, "Here I stand. I can do no other. So help me God."

The God Luther prayed to had been faithful many times before. And whether Luther would lose his life or keep it, he knew that his God would be faithful again.

Neither Wilberforce nor Luther could have stood against the evils and injustices of their times if they hadn't first learned to stand against the evil in their own hearts and in the hearts of those around them. We are no different.

Jesus said, "If anyone would come after me, let him deny himself and take up his cross and follow me. For whoever would save his life will lose it, but whoever loses his life for my sake and the gospel's will save it" (Mark 8:34–35).

Ultimately God is the One who gives us the strength to stand in any situation. But we must also recognize that much of that grace and strength is made available through the numerous opportunities He gives us on a daily basis to practice trusting Him enough to actually obey Him—even when it costs us something. Standing up for God in big, sometimes public, sometimes dangerous situations is made possible in part because we have stood up for God countless times before. Every time we do the right thing in God's name, we flex and build our muscles.

If we can't trust God with our popularity now, during high school, how will we ever trust Him with our lives on the mission field? If we can't stand for Him now in the classroom, how will we stand for Him in the courtroom, when it really matters?

Take a minute to think back through the stories and suggestions in this chapter and answer these questions:

- Is there a stand you know you should be taking but haven't?
- Is there something in your life you know is wrong but continue to do?

If a challenge comes to mind, don't ignore it. Take a first rebelutionary step. The hard thing you're contemplating may be the biggest, most difficult, and most rewarding hard thing you've ever done. Don't miss this good thing God is inviting you to do, and don't tell yourself it doesn't matter.

Doing what is right always matters—and it matters now.

PART 3

JOIN THE REBELUTION

GENERATION RISING

Creating a counterculture from scratch (and a dash of salt)

onner Cress was just a normal fifteen-year-old living a normal life on a normal spring day in Georgia when a magazine appeared in his family's mailbox from World Vision, an organization that focuses on relieving poverty and its effects around the globe.

Conner arrived home from school and headed upstairs to his room, snatching up any new magazines as he flew by the kitchen counter—just like he always did. Usually there were several. Today there was only one.

Normally Conner would just skim through the magazines looking for comics or contests, but this one seemed to suck him into every page. Ten minutes passed. Then twenty. Then thirty. An hour later, he was still sitting on the edge of his bed.

The magazine was a special edition on global poverty and featured page after page of haunting pictures. Little children, all skin and bones, stared out at Conner. Their shrunken bodies were shocking, but it was their eyes—big hollow eyes missing any spark of hope—that wouldn't let him go. Conner couldn't help wondering if the children in these pictures were even still alive. *Has anybody helped them? Does anybody care?*

The magazine took Conner on a journey through a world he never even knew existed, a world where over 1.1 billion people don't have access to clean water and where little children are pushed to such extreme dehydration that they can no longer cry tears. Everything inside Conner screamed, "This is not right!"

Suddenly his normal life seemed anything but normal. He felt like God was pointing at him and saying, "Look how blessed you are, Conner. Just look around and see how much I have blessed you with. Now what are you going to do about it?" At that point Conner knew his normal life had to change.

That was two years ago.

A BIGGER REALITY

Have you ever had an experience similar to the one Conner had that day? It's like walking through a door into another reality—one that is much different, much bigger, and much more unsettling than the world you had previously occupied. Your experience may have happened on a mission trip, or when you were reading about the number of abortions that take place in the United States every year, or when you saw a news clip showing children on the other side of the world chained to benches all day long rolling cigarettes.

Perhaps similar thoughts passed through your head:

- *I guess not getting invited to the party this weekend isn't such a big deal after all.*
- *I threw out more food yesterday than that kid will eat all week.*
- *Forgive me, God, for caring so much about stuff that doesn't even matter!*

Moments like that put our personal problems in perspective. They also demand a response. This chapter is about that response—exchanging our "normal," comfortable world for a bigger and very real world that rarely shows up in most of our homes. This chapter is about zooming out from a focus on personal rebelution (the Five Kinds of Hard things) to look at the Rebelution as a movement—a counterculture of like-minded young people whose efforts God can bless and who together can make history.

In this chapter we want to ask a very serious and exciting question: could it be that teenagers today are faced with a unique opportunity to do hard things—not just as individuals, but as a generation? And not just any hard things but big, history-shaping ones? To put it another way, could it be that our particular crop of young people has been placed on earth at this pivotal time in history for a reason?

Some people look at our generation and the challenges we face and despair. We don't. In every generation that faces intense challenges, God raises up those who will be His representatives to do His work. And often those representatives are young. We see this in Scripture, where young people like Joseph, Samuel, David, Josiah, Jeremiah, Esther, and Mary were chosen by God for the time in which they lived—and they changed the course of nations.

We believe the same thing is happening today. God is moving, and young people around the world are recognizing it and responding by overturning low expectations and doing hard things in creative, world-changing ways.

What happens when rebelutionaries band together to address the problems of their day? What is possible when a generation stops assuming that someone else will take care of the brokenness in the world—or that someone else will capitalize on current opportunities—and realizes that they are called to take action? What does it look like when a young person is passionate about what God is calling him or her to do—and that passion is contagious?

Jesus tells us what this God-honoring, world-changing counterculture would look like. In the gospels we find two simple but powerful word pictures of how a band of Christ followers really could impact an entire planet.

OPERATION SALT AND LIGHT

Jesus tells us,

> You are the salt of the earth. But if the salt loses its saltiness, how can it be made salty again? It is no longer good for anything, except to be thrown out and trampled by men.
>
> You are the light of the world. A city on a hill cannot be hidden. Neither do people light a lamp and put it under a bowl. Instead they put it on its stand, and it gives light to everyone in the house. In the same way, let your light shine before men, that they may see your good deeds and praise your Father in heaven. (Matthew 5:13–16, NIV)

In this passage, Jesus gives two different pictures of what it means to be His disciples, but both are addressed to all of us. We are salt. We are light. So what does that mean?

When we think about salt, our first thought is probably something along the lines of, *Gotta have some of that on my popcorn.* But Jesus isn't talking about salt like we use it today. Although salt was used to flavor food during the Roman era, its primary use was as a preservative. In a world without refrigerators or deep freezers, a little salt rubbed into meat would slow decay.

So when Jesus tells us we are "the salt of the earth," He's saying we have been placed here to preserve it until He returns—to fight against the decay of sin, to combat sickness and suffering, and to oppose corruption and injustice.

What about light? To be honest, the first thing we think about is the old Sunday-school song: "This little light of mine, I'm gonna let it shine." There's simple truth in that song, but it falls short of the full meaning of Jesus' words. In the Bible, light is often used to represent truth, especially the truth God has revealed in His Word. The picture of us as a city on a hill or a lamp on a stand means that as Christians we display the truth in word and action—shining the light of God's Word and the gospel all around us, in every corner.

In an address to students at the University of Notre Dame, the great apologist Francis Schaeffer made this profound statement:

> Christianity is not a series of truths in the plural, but
> rather truth spelled with a capital "T." Truth about total

reality, not just about religious things. Biblical Christianity is Truth concerning total reality—and the intellectual holding of that total Truth and then living in the light of that Truth.

That is what Jesus meant when He called us to be light. Where secular methods and philosophies hold sway in fields of business, education, the arts, or any other area of society and culture, we are called to bring biblical philosophies and methods founded on that "total Truth"—that's what it means to be light.

In both images, Jesus provides a model rebelutionaries can follow to impact the world around them. We are commissioned not just to love God and His Word but to radically impact our world with life and truth.

Putting the ideas of salt and light together gives countercultural rebelutionaries a clear mission statement: we are change makers who influence our world both as salt and light. That is to say, we influence our world both by *fighting against* sin, suffering, and decay and by *fighting for* truth and justice. And that covers a whole lot.

OH, THE THINGS WE WILL DO!

There is a misconception among some Christians that to "really live for Jesus" you have to go into the ministry, become a missionary, or marry someone who does. Those are high and noble callings, but to limit our idea of the radical Christian life to just a handful of areas isn't only wrong, it's dangerous.

The Rebelution needs Christians all over the world to be living as salt and light in business, science, medicine, law, politics, home-making and parenting, engineering, education, the arts, and every other field of endeavor. Like Schaeffer said, God's Word is Truth for all of life—and our unique makeup as individuals allows room for beautiful diversity within a generation committed to doing hard things for the glory of God.

The Rebelution needs Christian musicians. And we don't mean bands that talk about Jesus in all their songs, but musicians with a biblical view of culture and creativity who recognize areas of spiritual and moral decay in our generation and can impact their listeners with truth and life.

The Rebelution needs Christian men and women in business. By that we don't just mean people who tithe 10 percent of their income, pray before board meetings, and give money to missions. We need men and women who can champion a biblical view of business management and finances, who are committed to integrity, who have a heart to serve rather than take advantage, who do well by doing good instead of by cutting corners and working the system, and who are innovative in integrating their career with their calling—to be salt and light.

The Rebelution needs Christian filmmakers. By that we don't mean people who make films that always include a gospel invitation, but storytellers with a biblical worldview who know how to use the power of narrative to touch the gritty issues of life with the truth of God's Word.

These are just three examples out of many. A thriving Christian counterculture will fight poverty, heal disease, and expose corruption even as we earnestly fight against the sin and spiritual darkness at the root of all suffering. A generation of rebelutionaries will write books, direct films, raise and train children, design buildings, run for office, and make scientific and medical discoveries. We will strive to bring the truth of God's Word and the gospel to bear on every area of life we touch.

THE THREE PILLARS

You might've noticed that we skipped right past the clear warning in Jesus' words:

> If the salt loses its saltiness.... it is no longer good for
> anything, except to be thrown out and trampled by
> men. (Matthew 5:13, NIV)

"Thrown out and trampled" are sobering words. As we fight *against* sin, suffering, and corruption and fight *for* truth and justice, what is it that would dilute our effectiveness? What would shift the focus from God's glory to our own failures? What would make the watching world conclude that we're really no longer good for anything?

We think the answer is found in three power-packed words you've already encountered at various places in this book. They are so important, in fact, that we call these critical values the three pillars of the Rebelution: character, competence, and collaboration.

Being salt and light is the goal of rebelutionaries, but the three pillars are how we get there. Taken separately, each one certainly has merit, but only when all three work together can we build an effective and sustainable counterculture.

Think for a moment about how many Christian leaders, organizations, or causes have been discredited after one embarrassing failing or another. Most often they fail because they attempted to succeed without one or more of the pillars. For example:

- A pastor is an excellent speaker and leader but is weak in applying the truth of the gospel to his personal life. The pastor has competence but not character.
- A team of summer missionaries works hard to help the needy but a lack of coordination keeps them from accomplishing as much as they could have. The team has character but not collaboration.

- A business start-up brings together some of the best young engineers in the industry, but an underdeveloped business plan and budget shortfalls bring the promising enterprise to a screeching halt. The organization has collaboration but not competence.

Our vision for the Rebelution is to see these three qualities coming together in a new generation—young people who are passionate about growing in Christlikeness and sharing the gospel (character), who care deeply about skill, strategy, and creativity (competence), and who are committed to finding and working with a community of like-minded rebelutionaries (collaboration) to bring hope and healing to a lost and hurting world.

This alone is cause for excitement. And yet other generations have wanted to reach out and have been ineffective—even hurting their own cause through incompetence. Scores of Christian filmmakers, authors, politicians, businesspeople, artists, pastors, and leaders have failed miserably despite good intentions.

We still have confidence because we see rebelutionaries who are not only willing *to make* a difference, but are choosing to train themselves *to be* the difference. They remember that Jesus said, "Let your light shine before men, that they may see your good deeds and praise your Father in heaven" (Matthew 5:16, NIV).

Rebelutionaries know that competence matters for Christians because the Christian life is a life of action, and our actions are intended to result in God being glorified. They understand that the level of competence with which we perform the good works God has called us to do will determine how the watching world responds. They refuse to fall for the lie that says our Christian lives are meant to be lived behind closed doors—or tucked away at home when we leave for work or hang out with our friends.

And we see rebelutionaries melding humility of character with a zeal for collaboration—working together to accomplish greater things than they could ever do alone, inspiring and encouraging one another, bringing together diverse talents and resources, and taking advantage of modern technology to touch lives around the globe. We see young people working together to start businesses, launch organizations, and found ministries even though they live in different states, in different countries, or even on different continents.

We hope the potential and power of character, competence, and collaboration is as exciting to you as it is to us. But perhaps you feel discouraged that you don't see all three of these pillars operating in your life. Don't be.

The honest truth is that to balance your life on these three pillars requires constant work and consistent attention. And the good news is that the surefire way to build character and competence is to do hard things. Furthermore, the best way to attract people to come alongside you is to tackle a hard thing that is too big to accomplish alone.

Character, competence, and collaboration are the means by which our generation can fulfill its call to be salt and light—and keep from being "thrown out and trampled."

Now, with a portrait of the Rebelution counterculture in hand, let's take a look at the rest of Conner's story.

YEAR OF THE WORLD-CHANGER

For the rest of the spring, Conner couldn't stop thinking about that magazine and the photos that had grabbed his attention. Whenever he drank a glass of clean cool water, he thought of those African children walking miles every day for the equivalent of dirty swamp water. Whenever he threw away extra food because he was too stuffed to eat one more bite, he thought of their shrunken bodies that never had enough.

All summer he prayed, asking God to show him how he could help. But summer passed and there was still no answer.

Finally a simple idea flashed across his mind. *Why don't I make bracelets and sell them and use the money to dig wells in Africa?*

The idea seemed silly at first. He didn't know how much a well would cost. But when the idea wouldn't go away, Conner knew it was from God.

Once he had a plan it didn't take him long to get started. He knew he needed help, so he shared his vision with four friends—Dan Mirolli, Jared Ciervo, Kyle Blakely, and Logan Weber. They all signed up immediately. Kyle was seventeen, Dan had just turned sixteen, and everyone else was fifteen— all perfect ages, they decided, to change the world. They would pool their resources for the first batch of bracelets, then speak to churches and schools to raise money for wells and spread awareness about the need for clean water.

They named their organization Dry Tears. When we first met this band of brothers at our 2007 Rebelution conference in Denver, they had just come from being interviewed for *Breakaway* magazine's *Year of the World-Changer* series at Focus on the Family's national headquarters in Colorado Springs.

They told us that during the past year they had spoken to thousands of people about the need for clean water around the world. They had sold over thirty-five hundred bracelets and had branched out into selling T-shirts and water bottles as well. All told, they had raised over twenty thousand dollars— with over 90 percent of their sales coming from other teens. They could see their generation catching a passion for helping the afflicted and oppressed.

When we talked, they had already funded the construction of four different wells in Africa, plus an irrigation system that provides water for livestock and people, by working with the Blood:Water Mission, an organization started by the Chris-

tian music group Jars of Clay. According to that group's esti-
mates, the work of Dry Tears has provided clean water for over
twenty thousand people and saved hundreds of lives.

But these five young men aren't resting on their accomplishments. They're already looking to multiply their impact
by establishing student-led Dry Tears chapters around North
America.

DO YOU HAVE A HOLY AMBITION?

The Dry Tears guys are just a bunch of kids to some people.
But their drive to see their generation be salt and light to a
hurting world has allowed them to have a greater impact as
teenagers than most people have their whole lives. The difference isn't some special gifting—these are just normal guys
who are still terrified every time they have to speak in public.
The difference is that they have a holy ambition.

John Piper, pastor and author, defines a holy ambition as
something that you really, really, *really* want to do—and that
God wants you to do also. Some people would call this passion, but it's passion under the lordship of Jesus Christ. What's
yours?

At the beginning of this chapter we talked about opening
your heart and mind to a new, bigger reality. What questions,
thoughts, and crazy ideas have crossed your mind as you've
read? Has God begun to place a passion inside you to take

action on a larger scale—to do hard things that will launch you into the thick of the Christian counterculture we call the Rebelution?

If so, you're in a very exciting place. Getting hold of that kind of personal passion for the first time is often one of the primary passages between childhood and adulthood. Think of your holy ambition as a world-sized passion placed under the lordship of Jesus Christ. Open your heart to His world in all its broken beauty, praying that He will show you how you could be salt and light in the middle of it. He will.

In the next chapter, we're going to see how God has done it in the lives of seven other real-life rebelutionaries—a small but exciting taste of a growing movement.

A THOUSAND YOUNG HEROES

Stories of new beginnings, impossible challenges, and the teens who are living them

Looking out from backstage, fifteen-year-old Zach watched and listened as David Crowder led fifteen thousand concertgoers in a high-octane set of worship songs. It was the Del Mar Fairgrounds in sunny California, and to Zach the sea of concertgoers seemed to stretch out forever. They sang. They clapped. They danced in celebration, hands waving as they offered up praise. Zach mostly listened because, after the David Crowder Band, he was up next.

Rock stars take this stage, he thought. *High-school freshmen with a history of anxiety attacks and risk aversion don't. Shouldn't. Can't.*

"I don't think I can go up there," he muttered, but the words were lost in the thunderous worship, and no one heard.

Throughout this book we've asked what it would look like for our generation to start living out the principles of the Rebelution. The truth is that in many ways it's already happening. The movement is growing; a counterculture is emerging. And as you'll see in a minute, Zach Hunter is one of its leaders. Of course, he wouldn't call himself that. And as you probably gathered from the opening scene, Zach is definitely *not* doing what comes easily for him. He's just doing what God asks of him—passionately pursuing his holy ambition. Yes, it's been hard, but Zach now finds himself at the heart of a movement that is changing his world and yours. And he wouldn't turn back for all the comfort and ease in the world.

Zach isn't alone. Thousands of young people whose examples defy silly labels like "ordinary" or "exceptional" are creating a whole new set of expectations. They are rebels driven by a new kind of rebellion.

ZACH HUNTER: AN UNLIKELY HERO

When he was twelve years old, Zach Hunter was confronted with a painful fact: twenty-seven million people around the world still live in slavery. And half of them are children.

Zach's shocking encounter with that reality grew into a campaign against modern-day slavery that has taken this soft-spoken teen from the suburbs of Atlanta to the main stages of the nation's largest Christian musical festivals and far beyond.

"It was Black History Month," Zach recalls. "I'd been learning about people like Frederick Douglas and Harriet Tub-man, and I thought, *Man, if I'd lived back then, I would've done something to help them. I would've tried to end slavery and fight injustice.* And then when I found out there was still work to do, I realized I couldn't just stand around and wait for someone else to do something."

That's why three years before he'd be standing in the wings, watching David Crowder, Zach launched Loose Change to Loosen Chains (LC2LC), a campaign to raise money and awareness for the fight against modern-day slavery. The concept was simple: encourage his peers to gather and give their loose change, which then went to deserving organizations working to free slaves around the world.

Why loose change? Because there's literally tons of it between couch cushions, beneath car seats, and in the backs of sock drawers. Zach likes to point to an astounding estimate reported by *Real Simple* magazine that nearly $10.5 billion of loose change is just sitting around in American households—$10.5 billion! The Hunter family found nearly two hundred dollars worth in their own home.

LC2LC got started at Zach's church and school, raising almost ten thousand dollars in the initial drive. But this wasn't a one-time project for him. "In Isaiah 1:17, God charges us to rescue the oppressed and the orphan and to plead for the widow," Zach says. "It doesn't really get much more straightforward than that. It's a call to action from God."

"If you have a friend who likes snowboarding, you go snowboarding with him and it strengthens your relationship," he explains. "Well, God loves justice, so if you seek justice with God, you'll get to know Him better by being involved in something He cares about."

Soon Zach was tapped to become the global student spokesperson for the Amazing Change campaign in coordination with the film about William Wilberforce, *Amazing Grace,* and LC2LC spread to Australia, the United Kingdom, and Africa. With every step Zach became more and more convinced that God could use anyone to make a difference.

"Most people don't know that I struggled with an anxiety disorder almost up to the time I started speaking out about slavery," says Zach. "During these attacks I'd start feeling paranoid, have trouble breathing, or get extremely nauseated." Sometimes they'd get so bad that he'd just have to lie down till they passed. They robbed him of peace and nearly destroyed his confidence.

As he looked out at the huge crowd at the music festival, Zach felt those old fears come rushing back. David Crowder was wrapping up his set. It was Zach's moment. *Can I really speak in front of fifteen thousand people?*

Turning to his mom he urgently repeated, "I don't think I can go up there!"

To his surprise she replied, "That's okay. Then don't."

For a minute the battle raged inside the fearful fifteen-year-old. Then he stood up.

"No," he said firmly. "I have to go. If I don't speak up, no one will."

With his mom praying, Zach took the stage. Five minutes later, at his signal, the whole fairground erupted in a passionate cry for human dignity and justice on behalf of all those unable to raise their voices: "FREEDOM!" fifteen thousand voices roared.

Zach had found a cause that was bigger than his fear.

How far will Zach's holy ambition take him? Only time will tell. So far it has transformed a kid who suffers from anxiety attacks into a sixteen-year-old who has spoken to more than half a million people at live events, appeared on national television numerous times, written two books (*Be the Change* and *Generation Change*), and even delivered a speech at the White House.

Maybe that's why Zach loves the Old Testament stories where God chooses the most unlikely people to do His tasks: people like David, the runt of Jesse's sons; Jeremiah, the prophet who was too young to shave (okay, we're exaggerating); or Mary, the small-town girl who was chosen to be the mother of Jesus Christ.

"My dream is to see the end of slavery in my lifetime," Zach says, going on to quote the young British statesman William Pitt from the film *Amazing Grace:* "We're too young to know certain things are impossible, so we will do them anyway."

And because God is still in the business of choosing unlikely heroes to accomplish His big plans, Zach's impossible mission to change the world has already begun.

> We can make a difference in the lives of slaves. It doesn't really matter how young we are. It doesn't matter if we have physical, mental, or emotional disabilities. It doesn't matter the color of our skin or where we're from. Anybody can make a difference and be a voice for the voiceless.
>
> —Zach Hunter, age 16

JAZZY DYTES: SMALL VOICE, BIG WORLD

From grade school to high school, Jazzy Dytes built a reputation as one of the best young minds in Davao City, one of the largest cities in the Philippines. She was always her school's top representative at interschool competitions, and she always won. She was the essayist, the orator, the journalist, the debater, and the mathematician. As long as the world was spinning, Jazzy was winning prizes and praises. She was famous, she was great, she had everything—and she was only fifteen.

As the spotlight shone brighter, Jazzy became convinced that the only thing she didn't have was freedom from her parents' control. She had a brain and she believed she could live independently. Her opportunity arrived when she received a scholarship plus a living allowance from the University of the Philippines—the most prestigious university in the country. Only a week after turning sixteen, Jazzy was on campus. She was free.

Soon Jazzy had joined a sorority without her parents' knowledge. Her new friends drew her into political activism and a network of underground organizations. She rioted in the streets and marched against the system, condemning repression and denouncing commercialism. She learned to be a rebel for her country, fighting for something she didn't even understand. But this was her idea of what it meant to stand for her generation—rebellion. And she was so proud.

Completely free from her parents' oversight for the first time, Jazzy gave herself to her every desire. Soon she had a boyfriend—again without her parents' knowledge. Daryll was her "once in a lifetime," and they promised that they would always love each other. With her generous study allowance footing the bill, everything seemed to be at her fingertips. She was happy with her boyfriend. She was happy with her "stuff." She was happy rebelling. She was in control and she had everything she wanted. Then, only two months after entering university, her "perfect" world fell apart.

Jazzy Dytes disappeared.

On September 25, 2006, she was declared a "lost student" by the university and by police throughout the province. Soon word got out that Daryll was missing as well. When the couple finally emerged from hiding, they had missed final exams and their reputations were heavily damaged. But by then Jazzy didn't care.

"I was completely blinded by my rebellion," says Jazzy. "I was insane."

Her worried parents accepted her back with open arms, but she still considered them her greatest enemies. She continued to operate behind their backs, hiding the fact that her grades were plummeting because she was skipping classes to attend rallies and spend time with Daryll, whom they had forbidden her to see. When her parents finally asked the university for her transcripts, they were shocked by what they found.

Their brilliant daughter was failing in every subject except her favorites: trigonometry and chemistry. Jazzy had gone from being one of the top students at the university to one of the worst. Unable to hide the truth any longer, Jazzy broke down and confessed everything. Her parents immediately removed her from the university and brought her home, and the spotlight of attention that had followed her since grade school went out.

With her future seemingly shattered, Jazzy slipped into a deep depression. She was convinced that no one could ever forgive her for what she had done, and she could never forgive herself. She'd gone from someone everybody admired to the failure everyone gossiped about. She tried to commit suicide, but her brother caught her just in time. Afterward she couldn't even look at herself in the mirror.

One day, after nearly a month of isolation, Jazzy received a visit from a pastor's daughter. Eventually the conversation turned to God. The girl invited her to church and left her some Christian reading materials along with a link to a website called TheRebelution.com. Later that day Jazzy opened the first magazine and read the following words:

> It's possible to be so concerned with what has happened in the past, or so caught up in what's happening in the present, that we pay no attention to what God has for us next.

Jazzy began to read the Bible and two days later wrote an entry in her deserted journal. The entry was titled "God Loves

Me." That was when her smile began to return. She not only forgave herself, but she knew that God had forgiven her as well. She found the freedom she had been searching for all along—and it was through Jesus Christ. Ten days before turning seventeen, with her slate wiped clean and the spotlight gone, Jazzy Dytes had a new future to write. But she was no longer a rebel. She was a rebelutionary.

Never one to do things halfway, Jazzy threw herself into sharing Christ's love the same way she'd thrown herself into rioting and protesting. She committed to using the gifts that God had given her to serve and follow Him only. Within two months she was volunteering with two nongovernmental organizations as a children's rights advocate working with gangsters, sexually exploited girls, and abused children. The rebel without a cause now had a holy ambition. The angry activist had become the loving advocate.

"How do you engage a gang member in conversation?" Jazzy asked us not long ago in an e-mail. "How do you heal the soul of a sexually exploited young girl? For me there's no way. I just can't. I'm scared to mingle with them. I can't even look them straight in the eye. If it were up to me, I'd rather say, 'No thanks, God. You can look for someone else.' But it is God asking me. He has given me the desire to see these young people surrender their lives to Christ. Am I going to refuse God's calling because of fear and pride? Are they any more hopeless than I was?"

I will never stop seeking young people who don't yet know God. I will never stop chasing them, winning their souls to Christ. I believe that God will equip me with the strength and the right spirit. Deep inside me flows the DNA of a rebelutionary.

Even though I am just a young lady—a small voice in a big world—I believe I can do great things for God's glory. I am just a humble servant—geared up to face any challenge my Master sets before me.

—Jazzy Dytes, age 17

Brittany Lewin: A Calling Higher than Politics

When seventeen-year-old Brittany Lewin decided to attend a community breakfast in Weld County, Colorado, in late July 2006, she had no idea she would walk out as the campaign manager for a former U.S. congressman.

That particular breakfast featured Bob Schaffer, a Republican running for reelection to the state board of education. After hearing him speak, Brittany went up to Mr. Schaffer and asked if she could do anything to help his campaign. Never in a million years could she have predicted his response.

"Do you want to run it?" he asked.

On the ride home afterward, Brittany's mood alternated between laughing in amazement *(Is he really serious?)* and sober shock *(I have no idea how to do this)*. As soon as she got home, Brittany e-mailed Mr. Schaffer to make sure that he did, in fact, want a teenager managing his campaign. His response was immediate. Yes, he wanted a youth-led team.

He was serious.

Within an hour, Brittany was at the library checking out books on campaigning, scouring the Internet, and making leaflets. She had absolutely no idea what she was getting into, but she believed that God had opened a door, and she was determined to walk through it.

A subsequent planning meeting with Mr. Schaffer established several things. First, it would be an all-youth and only-youth campaign team—Brittany's friends, Rachael (nineteen) and Jenna (seventeen), could also join the team as volunteer coordinator and press secretary. Second, they would all call their boss "Bob" ("It still felt weird," Brittany says). Third, Brittany was the real, honest-to-goodness campaign manager—which was a full-time job.

The campaign's immediate projects included filing candidate paperwork, putting together a website, and designing campaign fliers. Since none of the teens had any experience managing campaigns, almost everything they did was a new learning experience—exciting yet often terrifying at the same time. Brittany's role, for example, required her to represent the campaign at numerous events, speaking publicly about

Bob Schaffer and giving campaign updates at political functions. She was responsible for staying on top of every detail of the campaign, from how much money was in the bank account to which events Bob was going to attend.

Looking back, Brittany can only laugh about the incredible variety her job entailed: "I oversaw the campaign's online presence, scripted campaign radio advertisements, wrote fund-raising letters, answered a billion phone calls and e-mails, did radio and newspaper interviews, and even co-hosted a radio show with two other all-youth campaign staffers. I really, *really* had to take everything one day at a time and one step at a time."

As if dealing with all of these new activities wasn't hard enough, Brittany also had to face skepticism because of her age. While many supported the idea of an all-youth campaign, others openly doubted that a seventeen-year-old could manage a campaign in a district the size of Indiana and a budget of fifty-five thousand dollars.

"There were definitely times when I thought it was impossible," Brittany admits. "But Bob really believed I could do it, and he told me so every day. Most important, I knew that God would give me everything I needed to complete the job He'd given me to do."

One of the team's largest tasks was to distribute eighty-five thousand copies of their campaign newspaper—the *Bob*

Schaffer Education Times. The student-authored paper included stories from the campaign trail, articles about Bob's experience, reports on the history and responsibility of the state board of education, and dozens of pictures showing teens participating in the campaign.

"You don't really realize what a large number eighty-five thousand is until you have to unload that many newspapers from the back of a U-Haul truck," Brittany says, laughing. "You should've seen the looks on my family's faces when I arrived home one day with twenty-five thousand newspapers that I needed to store somewhere."

As the election drew nearer, the campaign became more hectic, workdays stretched to over fourteen hours, and a general lack of sleep pervaded campaign headquarters. Brittany remembers telling her mom late one evening, "There are four hundred thousand voters in the Fourth Congressional District, and it's my job to make sure they all vote for Bob Schaffer."

She was joking—sort of.

Two and a half months after the Weld County breakfast, election day arrived, and the skeptics had their answer: Bob Schaffer's all-youth campaign had propelled him to a commanding win, with 57 percent of the vote. November 7, 2006, was victory day.

Looking back, Brittany is amazed at what she was able to accomplish, but in the end she doesn't consider it all that remarkable. "A lot of people, even U.S. senators and congress-men, have told me that what I did was special, but I really believe that other teens can not only do what I did, but that they can do much harder things."

Does Brittany have any regrets about how she's spent her teen years? Does she feel like she's missed out by not spending more time having fun? (Authors' tip: don't ask Brittany this question unless you want an incredibly passionate response.)

"Who ever said that doing hard things isn't fun?!" she explodes good-naturedly. "On the contrary, I feel I missed out by not aiming toward *more* hard things. You'll find more joy in doing what God has called you to do than a trip to the mall or a night at the movies will ever bring."

Brittany considers the opportunities she's had to work in politics a testimony to the marvelous plan of God for each and every person—if they are willing to follow Him wherever He leads, whatever the cost.

"The vision I have for the rest of my life is to live every day completely surrendered to God," Brittany told us over the phone. "I don't know what my future holds, but I know who holds the future." In the short-term, her future includes more politics. She's calling from the campaign headquarters of a leading presidential candidate.

"If I could give a peek into what I hope my life in the future will include..." She pauses. Then as if infused with a rush of confidence, the eighteen-year-old continues, "I'd describe the scene as a houseful of children, one on my lap as I hold the phone and discuss with some campaign manager what the next press release should say."

She laughs. Now that we've got her started, she's on a roll.

"As much as I love politics and campaigning, there is not a single political job I could find that would match the joy and satisfaction that comes from following God's special call to be a dedicated wife and mother. Campaigns are won and lost; elections happen every year. I can only do so much by myself. What's more inspiring to me is the thought of rebelutionaries across the world raising lots of counterculture, God-fearing, low-expectation-defying children who are constantly doing hard things for God's glory."

In the end, Brittany's heartfelt closing words—not her impressive political accomplishments—are the most countercultural thing of all.

> I believe that the doors God has opened for me and
> the lessons He has taught me through politics are
> only preparing me to be the wife and mother He
> wants me to be. Going from campaign manager to
> home manager sounds great to me. Being a wife and
> mother is a higher calling than politics.
>
> —Brittany Lewin, age 18

LESLIE AND LAUREN REAVELY: TAKING HOPE TO THE STREETS

At five thirty in the morning, Leslie and Lauren Reavely were jolted awake by fire alarms, smoke bombs, and the volunteer fire department. "Everyone take only your sleeping bags and shoes!" rescue workers shouted. "You are now refugees! The building has burned down, and you must leave immediately!"

The building wasn't actually on fire, as the girls soon figured out. But as the sisters and fifty other students were evacuated to a nearby field, it became easier and easier to imagine that they really were refugees.

Leslie and Lauren (ages fourteen and eleven) were participating in an annual summer program at Trout Lake, Washington, put on by WorldVenture. Each year's camp is designed to give young people a taste of what missionary life is like. The goal is to show students that God wants to use them to meet the physical and spiritual needs of people around the world. In Leslie and Lauren's case, the plan worked.

The next day and a half were spent living in a makeshift refugee camp. Everyone scavenged for peanuts scattered among the grass and found bananas tied to trees. They built shelters using tarps and cardboard boxes they pulled from a nearby dump. No one knew what would happen next, but no one was too worried about it. After all, it was missionary camp.

At the end of their first day as refugees, the students were told to stand in line to receive Operation Christmas Child shoe boxes that had been "flown in from America." The boxes contained simple items such as a toothbrush and toothpaste, a bar of soap, and a bottle of water.

A few days later, Leslie and Lauren found themselves back in their air-conditioned home in Portland, Oregon, enjoying their warm beds and a cold refrigerator crammed with plenty to eat. But the camp had been remarkably successful. They couldn't forget how good it had felt that night back at camp just to brush their teeth and wash their hands. They'd only lived as refugees for a day and a half. What about people who live like that for months or even years?

In the weeks that followed, the girls suddenly began noticing homeless men and women digging through Dumpsters and sleeping under bridges. Portland was the same, but Leslie and Lauren had changed. "We realized that homeless people are kind of like refugees in our own city," says Leslie. "They're refugees we are in a position to help."

In the past, the girls had never known quite how to serve the homeless. Lauren still remembers riding in the car with her mom when all they had to give a hungry man on the curb was a cantaloupe. "We didn't have any idea how he was going to eat it." Lauren blushes. "I'm not even sure if it was ripe."

But their experience at missionary camp had given them a fresh perspective—and an idea. After talking with their parents and a worker at the Portland Rescue Mission, the sisters launched Hope 2 Others (H2O), a ministry that provides homeless people with bags of essential items such as bottled water, granola bars, tuna and crackers, fruit snacks, Kleenex, hand wipes, a rescue mission meal voucher, and a gospel tract sharing the hope of Christ.

"Once a month we hold stuffing parties and have the bags available at our church," explains Leslie. The bags cost three dollars each, to cover the cost of the contents, and are intended for drivers to have in their cars so that when they meet a homeless person, they have a good solution to meet some of that person's needs.

The project has provided these "not necessarily shy, not necessarily outgoing" girls with many opportunities to trust God and step outside their comfort zones.

"I think the most stretching time for me was when we were first getting started," Leslie remembers. "Lauren and I had to speak about our idea to the elders of our church. I remember feeling the butterflies and being so nervous that I thought my voice wouldn't work! The meeting went well and now our ministry is up and running, but at that time I thought for sure it wouldn't happen. It was very nerve-racking for me!"

Since then, Leslie and Lauren (now sixteen and thirteen) have distributed close to five hundred bags and have been featured in the *Oregonian*—their state's largest newspaper.

"Teens open their hearts to Portland's homeless," read the headline.

Doug Hazen, director of the missionary camp that inspired them, was so impressed by their outreach that he invited them to speak at his organization's annual mission banquet and then structured the entire 2007 missionary camp around the theme of kids helping others.

"The Reavely girls were the inspiration for me," he says.

Because of all the attention, the girls have had to develop a strategy for dealing with the dozens of requests they receive from other groups wanting to launch similar ministries in their churches or schools.

"We've started handing out CDs on how to start your own H2O ministry and created a website—www.h2obags.com—where people can keep updated on our ministry," explains Lauren. "People we don't even know are helping with this outreach. It's beyond our wildest dreams."

Even with the success, the girls have often had to fight discouragement, whether because the bags aren't selling as fast as they would like or because someone questions their approach.

"At those times it seems like God always sends us encouragement from people who have been impacted by the ministry," Leslie says. "It's always a joy to hear from people who are excited about sharing God's love through our bags or to see the homeless people's reactions when they receive them."

One of their favorite stories to share is when they handed a bag to a homeless lady on an exit ramp and got to watch her open it as they waited for the light to change. She first pulled out the granola bar and then the gospel tract. To their excitement (okay, they were dancing in the car), she was reading it, and as they drove off she was *still* reading it!

"Our ultimate goal is to see hungry, homeless, and hopeless people find hope in Christ," says Lauren, "but we thought they didn't really read the tracts. Watching her take such interest in it reminded us that God *can* do anything."

In fact, learning to trust God to do the impossible through them has been the lesson of the entire process for Leslie and Lauren.

> Nothing is impossible with God! If you have a passion
> or a desire to do something for God, don't say, "It's
> impossible," and close the door with doubt or fear.
> God can do it, and He may want to do it through
> you! Don't underestimate Him. He can far exceed
> your expectations—I know that because He has
> done it for me.   —Leslie Reavely, age 16

BRANTLEY GUNN: MISSION FIELD NEXT DOOR

Whether it's smuggling Bibles into China, being robbed at gunpoint in Africa, or launching nonprofit organizations in

Jackson, Mississippi, sixteen-year-old Brantley Gunn sees himself as a normal teen who does slightly unusual things for a very good reason.

"Fulfilling the Great Commission has always been central in our family," says Brantley. "I remember even as a preschooler working with my family in the Salvation Army soup kitchens and distributing food parcels to poor families on holidays."

By age eleven Brantley was participating in short-term mission trips with his church. He still remembers lugging suitcases filled with Bibles through the streets of China with his dad. It was then that he first began to sense God calling him to a Great Commission lifestyle that would go beyond church-sponsored trips and other special occasions.

A year later Brantley found himself on another mission trip—this time to Kenya. His first impressions were of muddy streets, hovering flies, and dreary huts made out of a mixture of sticks and dried cow dung. One cramped hovel housed six people, two goats, a cow, and three dogs. Dung beetles were everywhere.

"I wish all of America's youth could go through just one day of an African experience," Brantley says. "The transformation would be powerful; I think it would motivate people to pursue heavenly treasures instead of material treasures."

Brantley's experience opened his eyes to the broken beauty of the world and taught him the importance of meeting both the physical and spiritual needs of people. "Jesus often treated an individual's physical needs before He attended to their spiritual needs," he explains. "After all, it's hard for a person to get serious about heaven if he's starving."

Returning home to Mississippi, Brantley's thoughts began to crystallize—even as his "new eyes" began to see the similarity between the African huts in Nairobi and the ramshackle houses in Jackson's ghettos. Some quick research confirmed his suspicions. He already lived among some of the worst poverty and urban rot in the United States.

Brantley Gunn's mission field was right outside his front door.

Armed with a holy ambition to serve "orphans and widows in their affliction" (James 1:27), Brantley launched Students Aiding Indigent Families (SAIF), a nonprofit charity to help needy families in Mississippi. SAIF purchases abandoned, dilapidated houses in Jackson's slums, then recruits teams of students to repair and remodel them into like-new condition. When the house is ready for sale, Brantley helps arrange bank financing for the new owner—usually a poor single mother.

Needless to say, getting such a serious operation started wasn't easy. Brantley spent hours researching how to set up a charity and met with other nonprofits, community service groups, and real estate investors. Three years since launching, SAIF has attracted more than two hundred students to the cause and generated over one hundred thousand dollars in annual revenue—but Brantley still remembers starting with no money, no members, and no experience.

"Any other thirteen-year-old facing such seemingly insurmountable obstacles would've thrown in the towel right there and left to play video games," says Steve Guyton, one of SAIF's adult board members, "but not Brantley. He has real grit."

Interestingly enough, Brantley would probably disagree. "I really don't think of myself as anything special or outstanding," he told us. In fact, he describes the attention he's received as "overwhelming" and "embarrassing." This from a guy who has long battled with ADD (attention deficit disorder) and being picked on at school because of his small size (though he happily reports a growth spurt over the last six months).

"I think most kids can do what I do," he says, "but most of them are more concerned with stuff like football and cheerleading. The only difference between them and me is that I focus on different things."

Of course, he clarifies, that doesn't mean he doesn't have any fun. Get him out on the motocross track and he can triple jump and thrust up with the best of them—and he's got the broken bones to prove it. But perhaps you could say his definition of *fun* is more inclusive—it includes serving others, making a difference, and pleasing God.

One of his favorite stories is about a woman named Hannah who lived in a rat- and roach-infested slum. She had two severely handicapped daughters and, somehow, lived off fifteen hundred dollars a month. SAIF found Hannah and set her family up in a remodeled three-bedroom home in a great neighborhood at a fraction of the cost of her old rent.

"When I handed Ms. Hannah the keys to her new home, she had a huge smile, and tears of joy were streaming down her face," says Brantley. "My shine reflects the smiles on the faces of people I help like Ms. Hannah—beams brighter than any sun."

> When I do my missionary work...it reminds me of
> what Eric Liddell says in the movie *Chariots of Fire:*
> "When I run, I feel God's pleasure." Well, when I do
> missionary work...I sense God's pleasure and feel like I
> am doing his will.... And for me that's what it means
> to live a full and fun life as a teenager.
>
> —Brantley Gunn, age 16

WHAT IS—AND WHAT COULD BE

"I think the low expectations the world puts on young people is the very thing that will lead our generation to do something huge," explains the nineteen-year-old excitedly, shifting position on the narrow coach. It's a nice tour bus, but it's no roomy lounge. "I really feel like intensity is growing in our generation. It's a passion that just needs to be unleashed on something that's right and pure."

As we sit in Leeland Mooring's tour bus just minutes before his Grammy-nominated band (that bears his first name) takes the stage at the Memorial Coliseum in Portland, it's hard not to feel like we've just discovered our long-lost triplet—discounting, of course, his reddish hair and musical genius (for some reason he's not asking us to join the band). Outward differences aside, his words match the pulse of everything we have to say.

"I think our generation is sick of the world," he continues. "They're sick of everything it has to offer. The only reason they're pursuing it is because that's all they're given—honestly. That's why our mission as a band is to wake up our generation. We want to see our generation doing hard things. We want them to be completely on fire for the gospel of Jesus Christ."

Are you sure we're not related?

Ever since we started on this remarkable journey two and a half years ago, we've been blown away time and again to hear the same heart-cry coming from young people all around the world—a growing restlessness that is finally finding its voice.

Leeland is right. Our generation *is* ready for an alternative. We *are* ready to do something big. In this chapter you've met some unlikely heroes who are already leading the way in redefining what the teen years are all about. They were twelve when they began to hate slavery, fourteen when they had compassion for the homeless, or seventeen when they decided that managing a fifty-five-thousand-dollar political campaign was not impossible.

Even though this chapter shows only a cross section of a much larger reality, we hope you've caught a glimpse of what is—and what could be. A generation is waking up—we can feel it. Rebelutionaries like Zach, Jazzy, Brittany, Leslie, Lauren, Brantley, and Leeland help us see it. This is real. It is happening.

Now it's time to write your story.

WORLD, MEET YOUR REBELUTIONARIES

Transforming your mission from a decision into a destiny

After a grueling two-hour hike, we finally reached the top of the ridge in Colorado's Front Range. The high walls of the gorge had blocked the spring sun on our way up, and our path had taken us back and forth across the canyon stream at least a dozen times. Both of us had managed to slip at least once on the icy stones, and the lower legs of our jeans were frozen stiff. Now heat from the sun began to warm our bodies as we took in the panorama.

It was breathtaking.

Below us we could see the old castle at Glen Eyrie surrounded by dark green forest. Beyond that lay the city of Colorado Springs, framed by a rich blue sky with a scattering of white clouds, and on our left, the jewel that is Garden of the Gods, with its towering red rock formations. The only thing rising above us was Pikes Peak, blanketed with snow. Even the hawks soared below us.

We carefully made our way to a narrow shelf of rock that jutted out over the canyon before settling down to rest, read our Bibles, and worship. Perched between earth and sky, we felt our smallness and God's unimaginable greatness.

That unforgettable morning came during a busy and stressful time. We had just finished launching the results from the Modesty Survey and were gearing up for our first national conference tour that summer. Even our trip to Colorado was Rebelution- and business-related. But as we sat there in the sun at the top of the world, our upcoming conferences suddenly didn't seem quite so overwhelming and we didn't feel quite so tired.

A good book can be like our experience on the mountain

that day. You are lifted out of the daily grind and transported to a new place. You spend time on the summit seeing things from a new perspective and with greater clarity. Your strength begins to come back and you're ready to return to the valley and live with fresh purpose.

We pray that this book has been that way for you. Like we said at the start, this is a different kind of teen book. It challenges you to embrace a better but harder way of living your teen years and beyond. We know that *Do Hard Things* is not an easy book with an easy message, but we've tried to do more than just talk about ideas. We wanted to show you the beauty of those ideas in action in the lives of young people around the world.

As you look back, we hope you'll see how far you've come.

First, we exposed the Myth of Adolescence and explored the true purpose of the teen years as our best opportunity to launch ourselves into an exciting future. Then we unpacked the rebelutionary mind-set of "do hard things" and broke it down into Five Kinds of Hard things that can change your world:

- things that take you outside your comfort zone—
  taking risks to grow
- things that go beyond what's expected or required—
  pursuing excellence

- things that are too big to accomplish alone—
  dreaming and daring big
- things that don't earn an immediate payoff—
  being faithful and choosing integrity
- things that go against the cultural norm—
  taking a stand for what is right

In the last few chapters we've stepped back and looked at the Rebelution as a movement. We asked what it would look like for a new generation to be salt and light by bringing together the three pillars of the Rebelution: Christlike character, God-honoring competence, and world-spanning collaboration. In the previous chapter we caught a glimpse of the inspiring stories already being written by this growing counterculture of rebelutionaries.

Now you've reached the summit, and we hope you have a personal vision for a new and exciting way of living. As you get ready to head back to the action-packed world of real life, we want to contribute a few thoughts to encourage and inspire you. Because real life is where you'll begin to create the most important story of this entire book: your own.

MAKING IT STICK

A mountaintop experience can get us excited. At the time, priorities are clear and the path ahead is easily visible. But once you start your descent, the excitement can fade. As you return to the valley, you start to see more obstacles and less of a view. You don't feel quite as invincible (or, as happened to one of us on the way down from our summit, you lose your footing and land hands first on a cactus).

Getting from big idea to meaningful change is tough.

So we have to ask: How can you make a successful transition from reading about big ideas to actually putting them into practice? How do you make what you've learned stick? And—worst-case scenario—how do you keep the majestic view in mind when you're digging cactus spines out of your hand?

The answer is to chart a clear course.

In this chapter we want to show you how to make your rebelution an experience that will endure and grow, an experience that God will bless. The following three examples won't match your real-world challenges exactly, but we think each story illustrates practical solutions for any rebelutionary who is ready to take his or her first steps.

Out with the Old

Noah is a high-school junior from Georgia. He has realized that for him, being a rebelutionary means finally getting serious about the unseen compromises in his life. His youth pastor recently gave a hard-hitting message on Hebrews 12:1: "Therefore, since we are surrounded by so great a cloud of witnesses, let us also lay aside every weight, and sin which clings so closely, and let us run with endurance the race that is set before us."

Noah knows that some weights in his life are keeping him from running his best race. His Halo addiction, for example. He's one of the better players he knows and for good reason— he plays almost every day, often late into the night. His grades suffer for it, and so do his friendships and family. In fact, besides going to church with his parents and his younger sister each week, he rarely spends time with them.

This isn't the first time Noah has felt convicted about these things. Last summer he went on a short-term mission trip to Mexico with his youth group. "After I got home I cut back on Halo for the rest of the summer," he says. "But once school started up, I don't know, I just kind of slipped back into old routines."

But this time is going to be different. "I know that if I really want to start doing hard things, I have to get rid of some old things first," he explains.

Step number one? "The Xbox has to go."

Here's Noah's five-step rebelutionary action plan:

1. *Put my Xbox 360 for sale on eBay.* Noah isn't saying he will never play Halo again, but he recognizes the need for a clean and total break. Plus, telling his friends at school that he got rid of his Xbox will give him a perfect opportunity to explain why he's doing it.

2. *Rearrange my room—literally.* Prior to this step, Noah's room was the Halo den. All the furniture was arranged to face the TV. Even the posters on the wall were for video games. Now the TV has been moved into the garage, and a lot of stuff has gone in the trash or been packed away in boxes. Noah has designed a "do hard things" poster for his door and cleared off his desk to make space for studying. The physical act of rearranging his room has helped reinforce his decision to be a rebelutionary.

3. *Talk to Pastor Jon about reading some good books.* Noah used to read a lot when he was younger but not so much lately. He decided to ask his pastor to recommend some good books from the church library.

4. *Spend personal time out with sis at least once a week.* Noah can remember the year he entered high school and the new challenges it brought—he'd always wished he had an older brother to teach him the ropes. Now his sister, Michelle, is going through the transition, and Noah wants to be there for her. Whether it's a run to Starbucks for coffee after school or a quick trip to the grocery store together, it will strengthen their relationship and give them time to talk.

5. *Join Dad or Mom on a work project at least twice
   a month.* Noah's father works around the house
   almost every weekend, but on the rare occasions
   when Noah has helped, he has tended toward a
   different room or the other side of the yard. Noah
   has decided to intentionally work *with* his dad so
   they can talk while they work. He'll be graduating
   in a few years, and he wants to get his dad's input
   on hard things he can do now to prepare for the
   future. He has the same plan for helping his mom
   in the kitchen.

Ask Noah and he'll tell you that he's more excited than
he's been in a long time. "Of course, it's just a start," he
admits. "But it's where I'm headed that matters. Recently I
haven't been headed anywhere! And even though sticking
with my plan will be hard at times, it will all be worth it.
That's what doing hard things is all about, right?"

HELPING THOSE WHO STAND ALONE

For Serena, being a rebelutionary means redeeming some
wasted years in terms of her sexual purity. She knows God
has forgiven her, and now her passion is to help other girls—
especially her fellow Latinas—avoid making the same mistakes she made. In her circles at school and work, she knows

girls who really don't want to give in to the cultural pressures in dress and relationships, but they don't know how to stand alone.

"So many girls out there are hurt and confused," Serena says. "Just like I was. I want to help launch a rebelution on this issue [of sexual purity]."

Serena has been going back and forth about launching a ministry on sexual purity for almost a month, and a lot of the details are still unclear to her. But she realizes that it's time to stop stalling and take the first step. If God has placed this holy ambition on her heart, He will help her accomplish it.

Here's Serena's five-step rebelutionary action plan:

1. *Call Mrs. Lopez and schedule a meeting for coffee, ASAP.* One person most responsible for helping Serena change her pattern of broken relationships was an older woman at her church. Mrs. Lopez met Serena at a music outreach event and had prayed and cried with her, sharing her own story of sin and redemption and connecting Serena with some new Christian friends. Now Serena wants to ask Mrs. Lopez to mentor her as she embarks on her rebelutionary adventure.

2. *Set up a blog and start writing articles.* Eventually Serena wants to have a full website with stories, articles, discussion forums, and a pledge for purity. Maybe she'll even have a print magazine. But for now the best way to get started is with a blog. She can link to

other websites in the sidebar and create an e-mail address so girls can contact her. The first articles will be her story and the lessons she's learned—soon she'll have other girls' stories to tell.

3. *IM [instant message] Nikki and ask if she'll help design a flier.* Nikki is a homeschooled rebelutionary from Pennsylvania and is great at graphic design. Serena has never met her in person, but they started messaging each other during a discussion about sexual purity on TheRebelution.com and have kept in touch. She knows Nikki will be glad to design a flier with a message from Serena and a link to her blog.

4. *Ask Sarah to help me spread the word at school.* Sarah is Serena's best friend and a total people person. We're told that *friendly* and *bubbly* don't begin to do her justice. Serena, on the other hand, is more reserved. The idea of handing out fliers scares her a bit—okay, more than a bit. If Sarah is with her, Serena will feel more confident—and she won't be able to chicken out.

5. *Find out what it takes to start a nonprofit organization.* Serena has heard that it's a bit of a process to become a government-recognized nonprofit, so she's going to do some research and find out what is involved. She won't need to be an "official" organization right away, but she's in this for the long haul and doesn't want to limit what God might do through her.

Serena has a holy ambition, and like most holy ambitions, it doesn't come with all the details figured out. "I honestly don't know what's going to happen," Serena says. "But I do know that nothing will happen until I trust God enough to take that first step."

RETHINKING COMPANIONSHIP

For fourteen-year-old Brandon, phase one of his rebelution is to completely reevaluate who he hangs out with. He was convicted when he read Proverbs 13:20 about walking "with the wise" or being the "companion of fools." He realizes that if he wants to rebel against low expectations and live radically for Christ, he is going to need friends who will encourage him to fight for that higher standard. He doesn't have that now.

In fact, Brandon has noticed that even his friends who say they're Christians don't really live like it. Even worse, lately he's caught himself being influenced by the jokes they tell and the language they use. He knows he can't talk like that at home, but he's started doing it at school in an effort to fit in. It has worked—his friends all laugh and slap him on the back—but fitting in isn't what Brandon wants anymore.

"Jesus said that it doesn't matter if you have the admiration of the world if you lose your soul," Brandon says slowly. "Do I want to please Jesus or my friends?"

Brandon has another insight: his companions aren't limited to people. "If foolish human companions harm you, aren't foolish movies or comic books just as bad?" he asks. "I'd never thought of them as 'friends' until now, but that's really what they are."

"Sometimes I spend more time with those companions than with my human friends," he admits. "And actually they're all pretty depressing."

Here's Brandon's five-step rebelutionary action plan:

1. *Talk to Dad and Mom about everything.* This one is the hardest thing on Brandon's list. That's why he put it first. He wants his parents to know what's been going on at school and what God has been doing in his heart. He knows that if he really wants to change, he will need their support and prayers.

2. *Talk to Jake and Logan at school tomorrow.* Jake and Logan are Brandon's best friends at school—and more than anything, he wants them to join him in rebelling against low expectations. He realizes that the first step in changing his friends is to change what kind of friend *he* is—and he plans to tell Jake and Logan about the Rebelution and invite them to read *Do Hard Things*.

3. *Invite Drew and Brady over this weekend.* Brandon knows that besides trying to be a wise companion to his old friends at school, he also needs to surround himself with new companions who will

help him keep on the right path. Drew and Brady are a year or two older than he is, but they're leaders in his youth group and introduced him to the Rebelution. They said they'd love for him to get more involved at church, and Brandon plans to take them up on it.

4. *Cut back on Internet use, except for projects.* This step is about those nonhuman companions: online videos, Manga, and games. Brandon recognizes that technology can be a tool or a toy depending on how you use it—but lately he's been using it to let in a lot of "foolish friends," and it's time to cut back. Plus, he says, being a rebelutionary will take all the extra time he can get. "And that's a good thing!" He laughs.

5. *Spend at least thirty minutes reading my Bible every day.* Brandon understands that more important than finding good companions is getting to know the Ultimate Companion—and there's no better way to do that than by reading His Word. Brandon doesn't know if he'll always be able to fit it in before school, but he's resolved to make it top priority by giving it the first free time he has each day. And cutting back on Internet time should help.

Brandon doesn't know what phase two of his rebelution will be for him yet, but he's confident that God will honor him if he remains humble.

"I'm the first rebelutionary I know of at my school," Brandon says, "but I know there are other teens who are looking for something more. Maybe I can help show them what that is."

THE STORY WAITING TO BE TOLD

Think about the rebelutionary path you believe God is calling *you* to take. As you read these three profiles, did any practical "first steps" pop into your mind? We noticed some recurring wisdom that Noah, Serena, and Brandon all applied to their own goals. For example,

- They identified what they needed to get honest about and to whom.
- They decided what negative actions or patterns needed to end.
- They recognized which people could best help them get from point A to point B and made a plan to get connected.
- They figured out one or two key action steps that, once taken, would make it a lot tougher for them to chicken out and turn back—and they decided when and how they would take the steps.
- They acknowledged that they couldn't succeed without God's help, so they made a practical plan to stay close to Him.

- They expected—and were already excited about—success!

People ask us where the Rebelution will be in ten years. We tell them we don't know the details—it's an impossible question to answer. But if enough teens follow the examples of Noah, Serena, and Brandon—and the scores of other rebelutionaries you've met in this book—we have no doubt that the message and impact of the Rebelution will only continue to spread and grow. Young people like you are only beginning to write the stories of their lives, carefully putting into action the vision from the mountaintop.

Someday, God willing, millions will hear and be inspired by the story that is waiting to be told. And that story is yours.

What is your five-step rebelutionary action plan to get started? Take a few minutes to write it down. Your words will be the record of your new beginning. Then join us and countless other young people on this adventure.

Yes, it will be hard. But we're rebelutionaries.

We do hard things.

AFTERWORD

What is the difference between a young person whose life is transformed by reading this book and a young person who remains mired in low expectations?" This question holds a special fascination for us as authors, but it should matter far more to you. The truths we've shared in this book can absolutely transform your life. But it's not automatic. Two people can read the same book. Both can get inspired. Both can be motivated to change. But often one succeeds and the other fails. One is changed forever and the other remains the same.

Instinctively, everyone wants to be the person who is changed. Whether we choose to read a book ourselves or someone else makes us read it, we would all like to be better off for having spent the time. And yet every single day millions of people engage with life-altering truths, feel that temporary surge of inspiration, and do nothing about it.

But let's keep this personal. Right now we're talking about you. And we're talking about this book, *Do Hard Things*. You've finished reading it. You've engaged with some powerful truths about what God expects of you. And the question you need to ask yourself is this: *Am I going to change or am I going to stay the same?*

This is a dangerous book, as are all books that inspire you to live differently. It would be better for you to have never read it than to read it and do nothing about it. The inspiration you feel is intended to give birth to action. Without action a sort of abortion takes place. And a tolerance for ignoring and even suppressing enthusiasm develops. Before you know it, you become a jaded and cynical grownup.

It is vitally important that you actually change. When you fail to act on inspiration, it isn't merely wasted—it turns to poison. A bit of youthful zeal dies. This is what C. S. Lewis meant in *The Screwtape Letters* when he wrote, "The more often [a person] feels without acting, the less he will be able ever to act, and, in the long run, the less he will be able to feel."

In order to help you turn your feelings into action, we'd like to share some stories. Real stories, in their own words, from young people who read *Do Hard Things* years ago and would honestly say it changed the course of their lives. These stories are also dangerous. They may raise the stakes by inspiring you even further—giving you a glimpse of where God could take you over the next few years. But they also contain the keys to channeling inspiration into life-changing, and even world-changing, action. Because that is precisely what each of these young people have done.

Our first story belongs to Priscilla, an eighteen-year-old author and evangelist from northern Minnesota, who read *Do Hard Things* six years ago as a self-professed shy and lazy tween.

When I was twelve years old, my older sisters told me I had to read *Do Hard Things*. I avoided it. The very title was convicting, and I didn't want my life to change. I was "happy" in the ruts of life and had no desire to do anything with the word *hard* attached.

Then I read the back of the book. I wanted to know what these Harris boys meant when they said that people didn't expect me to understand their message. I was upset at the idea that people thought I wasn't smart enough, so I decided to read the book. I read it in only a few days, and when I was done, I got on my knees and cried.

I wasn't used to crying because God had touched me, but as the tears flowed, I realized that I was wasting my life. I felt God calling me to be more than just a good kid. God was calling me to be a world changer.

How? I wondered. *How does someone as young as me do anything great for God?* I began to pray that God would show me something that I could do. It didn't start as a bang. God didn't reach down and make me governor. Instead, He helped me see that I was lazy. Did I change? Slowly. I still struggle with laziness, but I've found that God will help me if I ask.

I also began to realize that doing hard things is *hard*. I was beginning to lose my steam. I mean seriously, the world wasn't any different because I was trying to keep

my room clean. I flipped through *Do Hard Things*
again, and begged God to change my life.

Let's take a quick break from Priscilla's story to notice
something important. Priscilla asked God, no, *begged* God, to
change her life. She did so repeatedly over time. And as we'll
see in a minute, God answered her. Prayer is our most powerful tool, because transformation is always the work of God. Yet
many young people read this book, feel inspired, and forget to
come to God and plead with Him to make it mean something.
Any young person who genuinely wants to serve God and
change and grow for His glory should come confidently to
God in prayer and expect that God will answer in a wise and
timely way.

That is what happened for Priscilla. She was fighting her
laziness. She was praying, and she was waiting. Then God's
answer showed up in a small idea.

One day, I saw the movie *180* (www.180movie.com). It
has a strong pro-life message and closes with the gospel.
When I saw it, the idea struck me. *What if I could get
this movie into the hands of people all around my community?* I didn't know where to start, but after talking with
my mom, we decided to order ten copies of it.

For Valentine's Day, Dad and I went around to ten
of our neighbors and gave them a plate of valentine

cookies with a copy of the DVD. When I was done, I felt great. God had used me to do something *way* out of my comfort zone.

Then the idea grew. After talking it over with my Mom, I decided to order 250 copies. People thought I was weird, that I was just wasting my money, and that I would never get them all out. But we did.

Then I ordered one thousand DVDs. I felt like an idiot, but I wanted to do hard things. I wondered if people even watched the DVDs, if they even made a difference, but I also knew that I can't change lives; I can only give a message.

By God's grace, and with lots of help, we gave out every one of those DVDs. We gave them out at the fair, on Halloween, on the Fourth of July, during parades, and anywhere we could think of. We even gave one to a guy at a toll booth.

Not only did God allow us to give out every one of those DVDs, but we also gave out over one thousand gospel tracts. Did they make a difference? Did they change people's lives? I don't know. But it changed my life. I learned that doing hard things isn't about letting everyone see you. It's about serving God wherever you're called.

What am I doing now? Our church just ordered twelve hundred copies of another gospel DVD—and

I'm working on getting them out to people in need of Jesus Christ.

As Edward Everett Hale said, "I am only one, but I am one. I cannot do everything, but I can do something. And because I cannot do everything, I will not refuse to do the something that I can do."

I'm a normal teenager, but my God has called me on extraordinary adventures. Who would have ever guessed that God would use me? I'm the girl who's scared of strangers, and yet God has used me to knock on hundreds of doors. I'm scared of what people will think, and yet God allowed me to stand up in front of nearly two thousand people and share a strong evangelistic message. I'm scared of failure, and yet at the age of seventeen, I had my first three books published.

I'm not a super Christian, but I have a super God. A God who can use me and a God who calls me to do hard things.

—Priscilla Krahn, age 18
Minnesota

Priscilla's story is typical of how we've seen God use young people to change the world again and again. Over the course of her teenage years, she has shared the gospel with thousands of people. Who knows how many incredible stories she'll hear in heaven from men, women, and children who came to Christ after watching one of the DVDs she handed out? And yet it all started with a simple goal: to distribute ten DVDs in her own neighborhood.

Priscilla began her journey doing something that might seem small but took her outside her comfort zone and built some positive momentum. She worked her way up from ten DVDs to 250, then one thousand, and now twelve hundred. And each success paved the way for the next one. She built confidence. She gained experience.

Over the years we've seen many young people make the mistake of over-starting. They try to immediately run a marathon after being a lifelong couch potato. They try to raise twenty-five thousand dollars despite having no experience with fundraising. They try to distribute twelve hundred DVDs for their first project, rather than start with ten. Because they bite off more than they can chew, they tend to flounder and stall and get discouraged.

Failures and setbacks are part of doing hard things, as we'll see in our next story. But we don't want to set ourselves up to fail by over-starting. Trent is a sixteen-year-old from Florida who read *Do Hard Things* and was inspired to start a Bible study, preach his first sermon, go on a mission trip, and start a blog. Along the way he endured setbacks (and some painful flops), but he kept on going, and God has used him in some exciting ways.

We'll let him tell you about it.

Little did I know that my simple act of reading *Do Hard Things* would result in many people's lives changing. I was first compelled to read *Do Hard Things* because my youth group was having a book study on it. So, despite my reluctance to read "that boring nonfiction church stuff," I started it. From page 1 to the final chapter, I was super engaged. It shocked me how exciting and inspiring a "church book" could be.

Previously, I would dream and wish for many, many great things! I was, and still am, a big-time dreamer. The thing was, there was a problem stopping those dreams from becoming reality: the voice of apathy.

Whenever I had a big idea, it would tell me, *Snap back to reality, Trent! That's way out of your league. Stick with football and video games for now. At least that's easy. What you're planning takes WAYYYY too much effort. Have a sandwich instead...*

Normally I would forget about the hard and potentially life-changing idea. Then I read *Do Hard Things*.

This book inspired me beyond what I even thought possible. I began actually doing those hard things. I started my first Bible study, and I was so excited, but the first week, only one person came. The second week nobody came.

Was it discouraging? Yes. But, really, that didn't matter! I soon realized it was just training for my next assignment from God. I learned that sometimes the hard things we do don't work out the way we want them to. But that's okay, because sometimes they can change the world. You never know until you try!

Soon, my faith was stretched again, pulling me out of my comfort zone: I preached my first sermon for fifty middle school kids at a summer church event. When I gave the gospel invitation, three of those young teenagers received Jesus. It was amazing, but none of that would have happened if I never stepped outside my comfort zone.

One week after that, I was privileged to go to New York City to help at-risk kids in a poor neighborhood. There, we spent a week helping run a vacation Bible school to help keep the kids off the streets and share the gospel with them. Some even received Jesus right then and there! Those two weeks were the spiritual high of my life. I was happy that I was doing hard things for the kingdom of God. It was obvious, fun, exciting, and it was awesome.

But then life went back to normal, and I kept thinking, *What can I do?*

There was no sermon to preach. No mission trips to be a part of. No camp for youth group revival. Church was only two days a week. I was homeschooled…

So how in the world could I do hard things?

And then it hit me: *What if I started a blog?*

Immediately, those negative thoughts came flooding in: *Ha ha. Good one! Now back to reality, buddy. You know you can't handle that. It's too tough for you! Leave it to the pros...*

I pushed those thoughts away and started to think. *Alex and Brett did it, and God used them to impact millions. Why can't God use me too?*

So then I started a blog to inspire other young Christians to follow the Great Commission. I used a beginner's blogging site, and then I moved it to an official, full-fledged website.

Now, with close to twenty thousand views since the start and thousands of comments, God has used that project to impact many lives for Him. And I have a feeling that's just the beginning.

—Trent Blake, age 16

Florida

Trent discovered pretty quickly that doing hard things is actually *hard*. This shouldn't be a surprise to us, but it often is. Many young people give up when they hit bumps in the road, but Trent didn't do that. He viewed his failed Bible study as training. When the opportunity came to preach his first sermon, he jumped at it. He was still enthusiastic about doing hard things—and three young souls were eternally saved.

What's more, Trent wasn't content to return to normal life. As obvious opportunities to do hard things dried up, Trent made his own opportunities. He kept pushing himself outside his comfort zone. The result? His life and many others have been changed.

David's story takes this a step further. He's an Eagle Scout who works two jobs, is halfway through college, and is launching his own photography business. And he's only seventeen. He read *Do Hard Things* six years ago and has applied it to every area of his life.

Here's his story.

I was probably about eleven years old when I first read *Do Hard Things*. It was a point in my life when I knew I wasn't a little kid anymore, but I didn't feel like I fit in with the older kids. It turns out I would never feel like I fit in with the typical teenage crowd. Instead, I read *Do Hard Things* and was determined to not settle for mediocrity. I did everything I could to do hard things in my life, and over time those hard things paid off in ways I couldn't have imagined. It started with simple things, like trying to have a better attitude with my parents, and expanded to going far beyond my comfort zone.

One of the hardest things that I did was to become an Eagle Scout. It took years of hard work and dedication to complete this task. Along the way there were numerous hard things that could have easily stopped me, one of which was learning to swim. I never went near the deep end of the pool and I had always hated swimming lessons, but to become an Eagle Scout, I had to earn the swimming merit badge. Instead of letting this challenge overwhelm me, I decided to do the hard thing. I joined the swim team to force myself to learn how to swim.

When I was a teenager, school was a big part of my life. I set myself to doing hard things academically despite my general dislike of school. As I applied myself to doing my best, I discovered a love of learning. Because I was homeschooled, I was able to challenge myself by doing high-school level work in middle school. When I got to high school, it was time for me to go to a "real" school. I went to a private Christian high school, which had higher academic standards than the public schools nearby. To my surprise, I found that I wasn't challenged at school. Instead of letting my time go to waste, I challenged myself by playing, coaching, and refereeing soccer in my free time, along with finishing my Eagle Scout.

After I finished my first year, my family and I decided that I would not be challenged enough if I stayed. Instead, I was homeschooled again, and I took full-time college classes as a dual-credit student. In college I was able to find the level of academic rigor that I needed.

Although I was only fifteen at the time, I never let my age be an excuse for not working hard and doing well in my classes. I continued to work through high-school courses in the breaks between my college semesters, and I finished my last high-school graduation requirement the same day that I turned sixteen.

Now I am seventeen, have finished another year of college classes, and have found a passion in photography. A little less than a year ago, I started my photography business called Giant Killer Media. I am still taking college classes, and I am working two jobs to help me build my business. It's a lot of hard work, but if there is one thing I have learned, I have never regretted doing hard things.

Now I have given my copy of *Do Hard Things* to my ten-year-old sister. She is already doing hard things, like being my assistant on photography shoots. I know how much having an attitude of doing hard things has affected my life, and I am looking forward to seeing how it will affect hers.

—David Rhoads, age 17
Idaho

There are two ways to think about doing hard things. One is to think of them as something you occasionally *do*. The other is to think of them as something you *are*. Young people who aren't changed by this book tend to take the first approach. David takes the second approach. You can hear it in the way he describes doing hard things as an attitude. It isn't just an extra project he is adding to his life. It is a lifestyle. It is a mind-set he brings to all of life. And that mind-set keeps him from giving up on important goals or taking the easy way out, because this is who he *is*.

So where do you start? As you'll see in our final story—as well as in one of the appendixes to this book—doing hard things starts right where you are, with the challenges you face at home, at school, or at church. Now nineteen, Leah has already graduated from college, published a novel, and is a passionate advocate of adoption. But her journey of doing hard things started with playing the piano and learning an important lesson about comfort zones.

> When I was a young teenager, the book *Do Hard Things* made its way to my bookshelf. I don't remember exactly when or how, but I remember reading the first paragraph and feeling a thrill of anticipation. From page 1, I knew it would be a fun but challenging book to read, and I was right. What I didn't expect was the challenge of the chapter about small hard things. Small hard things seemed so much less important than the big stuff, but the book began to stretch my perspective. Comfort zones formed into barriers to be pushed and grown.
>
> Every time I read about small hard things and step-

ping outside of my comfort zone, one thing jumped to the forefront of my mind: playing the piano in public.

In my tiny church, our only pianist was aging. Failing eyesight made playing hymns harder and harder for her. She started coaxing me to play to get everyone to sit down so she could take over and play while everyone sang. Even with no one paying close attention, I shied away from her invitations. Playing the piano was definitely uncomfortable.

But suddenly my discomfort began to feel like a poor excuse. I started having mental arguments with myself. I didn't *have* to play the piano for my church. There was nothing wrong about feeling self-conscious about playing in front of other people. I made a lot of mistakes—a lot more than the older pianist. Those mistakes could trip up the singing congregation. On the other hand, I now realized that the only way to overcome discomfort was to step outside of my comfort zone and learn to do the uncomfortable task. Being uncomfortable was a symptom of growth.

I started to play before the church sang together. Then I began to practice in order to occasionally play a single hymn. My hands still got cold when I made mistakes. If someone complimented me on playing, I could inform them of exactly how many times I'd stumbled. But the comfort zone was being stretched.

Gradually, the discomfort began to fade. When the older pianist could no longer make it to church regularly, I was able to fill in. Another pianist came for a while, and I found myself somewhat reluctant to surrender the keyboard on Sunday mornings. When she phased out, I was happy to move back onto the piano bench.

My fingers still get cold when I make mistakes— trust me, I still make plenty of them—but playing hymns at church is no longer a task outside my comfort zone. Reading *Do Hard Things* helped prod me to take a step out of my comfort zone and learn to serve in a small way. It also taught me a bigger lesson: Comfort zones are not brick walls in life. They're more like balloons. When you try to inflate a balloon, it's hard to get it started. But after it starts to inflate, it gets easier to keep going. This lesson has continued to serve me well.

—Leah Good, age 19

Connecticut

Leah started right where she was with an obvious challenge. By focusing on something like playing the piano in public, she learned that her comfort zone could be successfully expanded. And that small victory paved the way for all her future achievements. As Leah puts it, "You never know just how long of a journey that first step will send you on."

So take your first step. Any step will do, no matter how

small. But it must take you outside your comfort zone. Your life can change, but you must take action. Like Priscilla, Trent, David, and Leah, you can use your teen years for serious ministry and real-world accomplishments. And it can start with one e-mail, a few conversations, or in Priscilla's case, ten DVDs. Nothing is stopping you. For the glory of God, just go for it.

DO HARD THINGS, THE GOSPEL, AND YOU

Hello, friend. Alex here. Yes, the book is done. Brett and I just want to share something with you that didn't quite fit elsewhere, something so important that these few pages could prove to be the most life-changing of all for you. Let me explain.

Do Hard Things is written by Christians to Christians, but it's not just for Christians. Maybe you have a Christian friend who gave it to you, or maybe you picked it up because the title caught your attention. Either way, I hope you enjoyed it and learned from it.

You don't have to believe in Jesus to benefit from doing hard things, just like you don't have to believe in Him to benefit from eating healthy food or from working out. It's the way life works because it's the way God made us. It's how *you* were created to grow.

My brother and I are Christians—unashamedly so. And we don't just settle for the label. Even though we often fail more than we succeed, we try to live our faith in every moment of every day, and we can see God working in our lives.

Because of that, we want to make sure all our readers, Christian or not, understand exactly where we're coming from with this book. Yes, doing hard things is not just for people who believe the Bible, but we would never have written this book or encouraged you to do hard things if we didn't have a Bible-shaped, gospel-driven view of life.

You've probably heard the word *gospel* many times before. It literally means "good news." But you may not be completely familiar with what this good news really is—even if you've grown up in church. So I want to tell you about this good news and explain how it relates to doing hard things and the Rebelution.

Our friend Mark Dever, who pastors a church in Washington DC, explains the good news using just four words: *God, man, Christ,* and *response.* Let's look at each of them.

THE GOOD NEWS

God is our all-wise, all-good, all-powerful Creator and Lord. He created us to glorify Him and enjoy His goodness forever. We're made to know Him personally.

> Worthy are you, our Lord and God, to receive glory
> and honor and power, for you created all things,
> and by your will they existed and were created.
> (Revelation 4:11)

> [Speaking to God] You make known to me the path
> of life; in your presence there is fullness of joy; at
> your right hand are pleasures forevermore.
> (Psalm 16:11)

Man is us—from Adam and Eve to you and me. We have rebelled against God by breaking His law (what the Bible calls sin) and pursuing the things of this world for our own selfish purposes, rather than for the purposes that God designed them. Our sin separates us from God and exposes us to His righteous judgment.

> All have sinned and fall short of the glory of God.
> (Romans 3:23)

> The wrath of God is revealed from heaven against all
> ungodliness and unrighteousness of men, who by their
> unrighteousness suppress the truth. (Romans 1:18)

Christ is our Savior. God sent His own Son down to earth to live a sinless life and die the death that we deserved. Through Jesus's death and resurrection, our debt is paid and our relationship with God can be restored in this life and for all eternity.

> For God so loved the world, that he gave his only Son,
> that whoever believes in him should not perish but
> have eternal life. (John 3:16)

> God shows his love for us in that while we were still
> sinners, Christ died for us. (Romans 5:8)

And finally, the only saving *response* to this greatest of good news is to repent of our sin and believe. That means turning away from what we know is wrong and turning to God, to trust and obey—professing that Jesus is our salvation and our Lord.

> Do you presume on the riches of his kindness and for-
> bearance and patience, not knowing that God's kind-
> ness is meant to lead you to repentance? (Romans 2:4)

If you confess with your mouth that Jesus is Lord and believe in your heart that God raised him from the dead, you will be saved. (Romans 10:9)

THE ULTIMATE HARD THING

What you just read is the gospel. This simple, profoundly beautiful truth has transformed millions of lives. Here is where the Rebelution comes in, because the mark of genuine transformation is to trust God enough to actually obey Him; to do what you know pleases Him, even when you know it won't please other people; to *do hard things*.

You see, we choose to do hard things because Jesus has done the hardest thing—the thing we could never do for ourselves: He died in our place and paid for our sins. Apart from Him, nothing we attempt or accomplish will have any enduring significance. But because He did something of *ultimate* significance, we can live lives that truly matter, not just for now, but for all eternity.

This truth allows us to confidently and joyfully do hard things, even at great cost to ourselves—for the honor of the One who saved us. Why? Because we know that the hard things we attempt will make a real difference. Our trust is not in the greatness of our vision or the strength of our effort, but in the grace and wisdom and goodness of God. Our reason for rebelling against low expectations in the world around us is that Jesus tells us He has overcome the world and—through faith in Him—so can we. As Philippians 4:13 says, we can do all things through Christ who strengthens us.

All of us—me, Brett, you—need what Christ did to save us. And not only to rescue us from the judgment we deserve, but also to keep us from wasting our lives on things that don't really matter. His salvation is a free gift—it only needs to be accepted.

Even if you've heard this before and are pretty sure you're already "saved," give these words careful thought. Being a Christian is so much more than the label you wear. It's about who (and what) you're living for. You can grow up in church and read your Bible every day, yet still not be living for God. In fact, you might be doing all those things just because it's *easier* to pretend that you're a Christian now around your family and friends than it would be to openly live for what you really care about.

Don't play games with God. Are you ready to repent and believe the good news of what Jesus has done for you? Will you join us in the most amazing adventure of all? If your answer is yes, here are some ideas of what to do next.

Talk to God

You can do this immediately; it doesn't matter where you are or what time it is. In your own words, tell God what's on your heart—that you're done with living for anything less than

Him. Don't worry about the words. He's there, He hears you, and He loves you as His own child.

Tell a Friend

Do you have any Christian family members or friends? Tell them what God has done in your heart and ask them to help mentor you and pray with you as you start out on the adventure of the Christian life.

Read the Bible

If you don't have your own Bible, ask a Christian friend to help you find one. Finding one won't be hard. Once you have one, start by reading in the Gospels: Matthew, Mark, Luke, and John. Get to know Jesus.

Find a Church

All Christians, especially new ones, need the fellowship and support of other believers in a local church. The pastor, youth pastor, or other adults will be able to help answer questions you might have—and the church can be a source of new friends who are passionate about living for God.

Join the Rebelution

Get plugged in to TheRebelution.com and get to know like-minded rebelutionaries around the world. Share your story with us (see the About the Authors page). We'd love to hear it.

Now that you are a Christian, you may also want to reread parts of this book. Plus, look for opportunities to share the gospel with your friends—maybe even by giving them a copy of *Do Hard Things* or by starting a study group at your school.

———————

Thanks for reading what I had to say. If it changes one life, this whole book will have been worth it. God bless!

QUESTIONS (AND STORIES) TO GET YOU STARTED

Adapted from *Start Here: Doing Hard Things Right Where You Are*

If you're feeling lost in trying to figure out where to start, you might be asking practical questions about how to create a plan, get others involved, and make your project work.

Those are good questions, and we tackle all of them (and more) in our book *Start Here*. But most of the time, those *aren't* the right questions to be asking—at least not at first.

The best question to ask right at the beginning is "*Why am I doing hard things?*" When we remember that we're doing hard things to glorify God and become more of who He created us to be, it puts the "How do I start?" question in a different light.

As you think and pray about what God wants *you* to be doing, keep in mind that you don't have to fight God in order to do hard things. He *wants* you to do hard things! The Bible says that He has prepared good works for you and has prepared you for those good works (see Ephesians 2:10). God is far more concerned about His glory, your good, and the good of those around you than you are. That means you don't have to engineer something—you can trust Him, be faithful, and be ready for *His* timing.

So here are some thoughts on responding to what God is already eager to do in your life.

I'm Ready to Get Started—on Something! What Do I Do Now?

When we think or talk about doing hard things, it's easy to think only about the big stuff. If we assume being a rebelutionary means fighting slavery, digging wells in Africa, running a political campaign, or writing a book, then it *is* hard to know where to begin!

But if our goal is to glorify God—to point other people to Him and show more of what *He* can do—then our first priority is to be faithful with what He's *already given us to do,* not embark on a big new adventure. *What* we're doing doesn't necessarily change right away, but *how* and *why* we're doing it will change dramatically.

Let us introduce you to the first of many real-life stories we share in *Start Here.* As you'll see in Elisabeth's story, the place we start doing hard things is right where God has us already—such as sitting in a car on a snowy night.

I was ready to go out and conquer hard projects. Big responsibilities. Things far outside my comfort zone. I prayed for God to work through me in big ways. He answered me, but not quite in ways I expected.

For instance, one night on the way home in a blizzard, my dad stopped for a few minutes to pick up some necessities at the store. I waited in the car and surveyed the nearly empty parking lot until my eye caught a lone car with a person scraping off snow. As I looked closer, I saw that it was an elderly lady trying to scrape off her car while leaning on a cane. She wasn't making much progress because the snow was falling faster than she could wipe it off. I felt instinctively that

I had to help her. I ran out with my scraper, and soon a few other people joined me in clearing off her car.

Nothing outwardly significant happened then, but this was the first time I had strongly heard God's voice and responded to it. As I tuned in, I began to recognize His voice at other times. I sensed that I should go talk to the girl who was crying in the bathroom at school— it turns out she was pregnant and needed help. Or that I should offer tips to someone who was trying out for the sports team—it turns out she needed advice on deeper areas of her life that she normally wouldn't have opened up about.

What I have found is that in order to do hard things and conquer big challenges, we need to be willing to listen to that little voice the Holy Spirit uses. The more you listen, the clearer it becomes. And in order to do the great thing, you must first be a servant.

—Elisabeth, age 17
Raymond, Maine

Even though Elisabeth had dreams about the hard things *she* wanted to be doing, she was tuned in to God's voice when He spoke. God answered her in ways she didn't expect, but she was ready to hear Him. And with one simple act of obedience, Elisabeth became aware of many other opportunities for doing hard things.

When your heart and mind are alert, you can see opportunities to do *hard things* in the *everyday things*. It might start with a renewed commitment to excellence in your schoolwork or a decision to help more around the house. School and chores are things you probably do already, but now, as a rebelutionary, you are doing them with a new attitude. Your primary goal isn't to do something extraordinary but to do all things, even the ordinary things, extraordinarily well.

We want rebelutionaries to dream big, but we've also observed that God often passes over the person with grand, me-focused plans in favor of the one who has a heart to love others, to trust Him, and to do the small things for their own sake.

Doing hard things doesn't mean being preoccupied with something bigger, different, and more exciting all the time. It means being ready and willing to obey, no matter how big, small, or hard it might be. Elisabeth's openness to God's leading made her available in several unexpected opportunities to show the love of Christ. Faithfulness in small hard things is always the fuel for bigger hard things.

If we say we want to do hard things for God, but we're not satisfied with pursuing excellence where He has placed us (at home, at school, and at work), it's likely that we're really more interested in getting glory for ourselves than in getting glory for Him.

So, where do you start? Right where you are—with a new attitude, a new heart, and a new mind open to the everyday hard things available to you right now. They will lead you to the next step.

DO SMALL HARD THINGS REALLY COUNT?

To answer this question, take out the word *small*. Do hard things really count? Of course! Remember, *small doesn't mean easy*. We should still be stepping outside our comfort zones, going above and beyond expectations, and doing what's right, even if our actions don't seem all that impressive to most people. Why? Because big or small, the hard things God calls us to do are about Him, not us.

That's why, to fully answer the question, we have to ask a bigger one: what *ultimately* counts? If the answer is "being famous" or "what people think about me," then small hard things don't matter much. But when we read God's Word, we find that small things have great significance, not just to prepare us for bigger things but also for their own sake. And sometimes small hard things are the hardest things of all.

In Colossians 3:23, Paul writes, "Whatever you do, work at it with all your heart, as working for the Lord, not for men" (NIV). In 1 Corinthians 10:31, he writes, "Whether you eat or drink or *whatever you do,* do it all for the glory of God" (NIV). What Paul is saying is that everything—even something as simple as befriending someone in gym class—can be done for God's glory. And that means *nothing* we do for God is insignificant.

This year I started attending a new public high school. It was in one of my PE classes during the first month of school that I began noticing the "outsiders." As part of the class, we had to warm up by running five or six laps around the school track. For most of the kids in the class, including me, this was no problem. But not everyone was in the greatest shape after a long summer.

After finishing my laps, I was standing around and saw a girl who was behind everyone else. She was struggling to keep up. At first I didn't give her a second thought, but as I saw how much she was hurting, the Lord put her on my heart. I sensed that God was saying, *Hannah, I want you to go run with her!*

I felt really, really weird. I immediately argued back, *What, Jesus? Are You serious? I've never even spoken to that girl! I don't even know her name!* But I knew I had to obey Him, even though everyone else in the class might think I was dumb.

So, saying a silent prayer, I jogged out to the girl. She was crying and struggling to breathe, but her face radiated with surprise and thankfulness as I came up beside her. Even though I didn't know her, the love of the Lord brought us together, and we finished those laps strong.

—Hannah, age 17
Chesapeake, Virginia

We doubt anyone in Hannah's class patted her on the back, and her story certainly didn't make the newspaper. Was it still worth it? It depends on how you answer the question we asked earlier: what ultimately counts?

The Westminster Shorter Catechism (an early Q and A about Christian beliefs) says, "What is the chief end of man? To glorify God, and enjoy Him forever." That means that simple acts of obedience, like Hannah's, matter a lot. It also means that it's possible to dazzle people with the hard things we do and still waste our lives if we're doing those things only to impress others and bring glory to ourselves.

Small hard things might have "small" results in this life, but as Paul encourages us, "Let us not grow weary of doing good, for in due season we will reap, if we do not give up" (Galatians 6:9). God will bring a harvest—whether in this life or the next—if we persevere in the everyday things He has given us to do, at school and at home.

Do you feel God calling you to do something big for Him? Don't despise the day of small beginnings. Not only are big hard things usually made up of a lot small hard things put together (so you're getting good practice!), but also God has a way of opening new opportunities when we least expect it.

Big hard things often start with one small step. Just ask Jaime Coleman.

A few years ago, Jaime's church partnered with a missions organization that uses humanitarian projects to share the gospel in rural Kenyan communities. Her church adopted the town of Karogoto, and Jaime soon discovered a pressing need in the town for something that most of us take for granted: shoes.

Jaime figured that her family wasn't the only one with shoes in the closet they didn't need. She set a goal to collect 150 pairs of shoes. Her plan was to kick off the drive with a Barefoot Mile at her high school's track. People would come, donate shoes, and walk four laps around the track barefoot. Some adults questioned whether anyone would show up—but it didn't take God long to prove them wrong.

"There were definitely low expectations," Jaime told us. "It was discouraging, but I knew God could make it happen. On a rainy Saturday, fifty people showed up at the track—with 1,164 pairs of shoes! By the time the drive was over, God had brought in over 4,200 pairs of shoes for the people of Karogoto."

Why do we share Jaime's story in response to a question about "small" hard things? Because Jaime didn't set out to collect 4,200 pairs of shoes. Her desire was to participate in the work of her local church. Her goal was small: 150 pairs of shoes. And even now, when we talk to her, she refuses to take credit for what God has done.

Stories like Jaime's remind us that God wants (and will use) faith, humility, and availability—not glory-seeking, pride, or a preoccupation with our own ideas. If Jaime had thought,

A few dozen pairs of shoes isn't going to make enough of a difference, she would have missed a chance to see God do *incredible* things with a simple idea. If Hannah had second-guessed God's prompting to do a "small" hard thing in gym class that day, she would have missed an opportunity to show His love to someone else.

Nothing we do for God is insignificant. When we have this as our mind-set, then we won't get proud if God allows us to do something big and we won't get discouraged if we feel stuck in the small things. Remember, neither fame nor obscurity is the goal. The goal is obedience to God, effectiveness in whatever He gives us to do, and a heart that glorifies Him.

Whether we are called to live life on a big stage or behind the scenes, we cannot forget the words of Jesus, who modeled this mind-set for us: "The greatest among you shall be your servant. Whoever exalts himself will be humbled, and whoever humbles himself will be exalted" (Matthew 23:11–12).

If these questions and answers helped you, consider picking up a copy of our second book, *Start Here: Doing Hard Things Right Where You Are.* It is jam-packed with stories and insights in response to nearly thirty of the most common questions we receive from teens around the world. We tackle subjects like pride, discouragement, time management, entertainment, and friendship—all the way down to the nitty-gritty of fundraising for projects, handling media interviews, and getting your local church involved with your cause.

Do Hard Things is the manifesto, but *Start Here* is the field guide. If you're ready to take the next step and blast past mediocrity for the glory of God—get *Start Here*.

You'll be glad you did.

100 HARD THINGS

We love the fact that rebelutionaries are doing far too many hard things to include all their stories in our books. But as an excuse to share some more—and to get you started in figuring out what hard thing to tackle next—here are one hundred real-life examples of hard things young people like you have done. For more ideas or to share your own, "like" the Rebelution on Facebook or follow us on Twitter (@therebelution).

1. Sent post cards to shut-ins at my church.
2. Memorized a whole book of the Bible.
3. Called my dad on his birthday after my parents got divorced.

4. Made care packages for members of the military.
5. Didn't text for a week and used my extra time to read the Bible.
6. Worked up to one hundred push-ups in four weeks.
7. Saved my first kiss for my wedding day.
8. Made meals for a new mom and cleaned her kitchen while she slept.
9. Sold all the clothes I didn't need and gave the money to charity.
10. Made small gifts and distributed them at a nursing home on Christmas Eve.
11. Let my brother win an argument.
12. Wrote a note of encouragement to the principal of my school.
13. Kept a daily journal of what God was teaching me over a year.
14. Put on a concert at church and raised two thousand dollars for a missionary family in Mexico.
15. Asked my parents to come to church with me.
16. Wrote a song and recorded it in a studio.
17. Hosted a Bible study for kids in my neighborhood.
18. Got certified with the American Heart Association to perform CPR and first aid.
19. Started teaching piano lessons.
20. Learned Spanish.
21. Worked as a camp counselor for kids with disabilities.

22. Donated ten inches of hair to Locks of Love—twice!

23. Sponsored a child through Compassion International (Compassion.com).

24. Ran a marathon.

25. Volunteered on a political campaign.

26. Stopped spending money on fast food and coffee and then donated that money to an orphanage.

27. Started a dance and drama team at my church.

28. Fasted from TV for a month.

29. Donated blood to the Red Cross.

30. Wrote a letter to the editor of my local paper.

31. Served as a nursery volunteer in my church.

32. Was the team leader of the Relay for Life for the American Cancer Society (Cancer.org).

33. Apologized.

34. Read a book out loud to my younger siblings.

35. Went on a mission trip to an Indian reservation.

36. Moved away from home to be near my ill brother.

37. Started a book club for young women in my church.

38. Rode one thousand miles on my bicycle in six months.

39. Planned and led a rim-to-rim Grand Canyon backpacking trip.

40. Took banana bread to our neighbors.

41. Repaired my relationship with my mom.

42. Invited someone I find annoying to hang out with me and my friends.

43. Volunteered once a week for an elementary-school tutoring program.
44. Designed and made modest but fashionable clothes.
45. Started an overseas adoption ministry at my church.
46. Prayed out loud in a group.
47. Wrote to persecuted Christians through PrisonerAlert .com.
48. Wrote letters to representatives in Congress.
49. Prayed with someone in the school hallway.
50. Practiced my musical instrument every day.
51. Started an after-school Bible club in a public elementary school.
52. Sat with a widow at church who had been sitting alone.
53. Ran errands for my parents.
54. Wrote an encouraging letter to my youth pastor.
55. Stopped complaining.
56. Set a bedtime for myself and kept to it.
57. Asked my pastor a question that's been bothering me even though I felt silly.
58. Kept up with the news and prayed about world events.
59. Asked an older Christian friend what area she thought I needed to grow in most.
60. Wrote my parents a letter thanking them for all they do.
61. Took notes at church and reviewed them during the week.

62. Wrote down long-term goals for my life and prayed about them regularly.

63. Gave up my Saturday morning sleep-ins to volunteer at a soup kitchen.

64. Started a regular exercise program.

65. Made over one hundred and fifty apple pies (twice) for a mission trip fund-raiser.

66. Started a pro-life group at my school.

67. Stopped gossiping.

68. Organized a group of friends to pick up trash in my neighborhood.

69. Collected used baby items and donated them to a crisis pregnancy center.

70. Supported a family member who struggles with depression.

71. Learned guitar and accompanied my youth group's praise choir.

72. Asked my friends not to curse around me.

73. Prayed for the kid at school who mistreats me.

74. Bought a carnation from a woman on the street and talked with her.

75. Trained with Child Evangelism Fellowship (CEFonline .com).

76. Baby-sat for a single mom who couldn't pay me much.

77. Started an organization that buys ultrasound machines for pregnancy centers.

78. Led See You at the Pole at my school (SYATP.com).

79. Started an evangelistic Bible study for my volleyball team.

80. Hosted a 30 Hour Famine through World Vision (WorldVision.org).

81. Volunteered in an after-school program at a homeless shelter.

82. Tutored four children while their mom recovered from a stroke.

83. Asked my stepsister out for a soda even though we don't get along.

84. Stopped making mean and sarcastic jokes.

85. Set a budget for my finances and stuck to it.

86. Started my own flower business.

87. Played guitar for hospice patients.

88. Took a group of younger kids to a fast-food place and talked about Christ.

89. Organized citywide baby showers for a crisis pregnancy center.

90. Got up earlier than usual in the morning to read my Bible.

91. Set up a prayer station in a city park and offered to pray for people.

92. Asked local businesses if I could volunteer my time to help them.

93. Became an AWANA leader (Awana.org).

94. Befriended an exchange student at college.
95. Ended a relationship that wasn't healthy.
96. Refused a part in a play because certain lines in the script violated my conscience.
97. Made an extra plate of food to take to an elderly neighbor.
98. Raised an assistance dog through Guide Dogs of America (GuideDogsofAmerica.org).
99. Shared a meal with a homeless man and listened to his story.
100. Competed in the National Bible Bee (BibleBee.org).

CONVERSATION GUIDE

I f you're like us, talking with others about what you're reading helps you decide what you think and how to respond to what a book is saying. This chapter-by-chapter study guide is intended to help you do just that. Use it for personal study, if you wish, but we think it works best in a group. And the best group is one where you're surrounded by others who care about the same things you do and are ready to put truth into action.

Don't feel you have to process every question. It's not a test, and as often as not, there's no one right answer. Also, don't let our questions limit what you ask or where you go. Ask God to direct your thoughts and decisions. And ask Him for courage—lots of it. Because big ideas are weak ideas if we're not willing to let them shape how we think and live. So use this study guide to zero in on the ideas, choices, and actions that seem most promising and helpful to you and your friends. Then expect great things to happen in your lives as you do hard things for the glory of God!

Your fellow rebelutionaries,

Alex and Brett Harris

1 MOST PEOPLE DON'T...
A different kind of teen book

"We believe our generation is ready to rethink what teens are capable of doing and becoming." With that statement, the authors set the stage for a discussion about doing things differently. Then they identify the unique angle of *Do Hard Things:* instead of being a book where adults tell teens how to change, it's a conversation among teens who are ready to lead the way.

Questions for Discussion and Reflection

1. Usually we try to look to older (hopefully wiser) people for life advice. Do you see any risks when teenagers—in this case, two nineteen-year-olds—try to persuade other young people to change how they think? On the other hand, what might be some advantages to the authors' age?

2. Have you ever read a book or listened to a message that seemed dumbed down—as if you and your peers couldn't handle something more substantial? Does this bother you?

3. In what ways do you think popular culture misrepresents what the teen years are for? Can you think of one thing that would change if you and your friends believed—really believed—that low expectations were ripping you off?

2 THE BIRTH OF A BIG IDEA
Rumblings of a rebelution

In this chapter, Alex and Brett tell the story of their journey from being bored teens to being Supreme Court interns, campaign workers, and blog hosts. But before they had new experiences, they had new ideas—big ideas like:

- Our generation is getting robbed!
- There has to be more to the teen years than goofing off.
- Ordinary teens can make a big difference in the world.

They close the chapter by inviting readers to join them in an uprising "against a cultural mind-set that twists the purpose and potential of the teen years and threatens to cripple our generation."

Questions for Discussion and Reflection

1. Looking back, do you see a season, a book, or an event that changed what you believe or how you live? If so, talk about it. How are you different now?

2. One teen told Alex and Brett, "Everyone I know at school is shackled by low expectations." Could you say the same thing? If so, talk about why.

3. History shows that youth movements against God-established authority have generally not amounted to much. How do the authors set their message apart from such movements?

3 THE MYTH OF ADOLESCENCE
Exposing expectations that are robbing our generation

An elephant is an incredibly powerful beast that can be restrained by a piece of twine. (No kidding.) And that powerful animal just might be you, say Alex and Brett. Why? Because teens today buy into "the Myth of Adolescence." That myth is an assumption that the teen years can't add up to much and are meant to be spent as some sort of vacation from responsibility. Unfortunately, those low expectations end up trapping and limiting teens for no good reason. But it doesn't have to be that way. Even the word teenager, the authors point out, is a recent invention. We can choose to live by higher standards. We can leave childish ways behind and grow up. We can decide to do hard things. That, say the twins, is where the Rebelution starts.

Questions for Discussion and Reflection

1. Do you think that harmless-sounding lies about the teen years could be holding back both you and other teens you know? Talk about it.

2. What do your parents expect you to do at home in an average week? Do you deliver? Be honest. How much time and effort does it take to do what's asked of you? Do you think your parents require too much or too little?

3. Have you ever found yourself behaving very differently—and accomplishing a lot more—simply because someone expected you to? Describe the experience.

4 A BETTER WAY
Reclaiming the teen years as the launching pad of life

This chapter starts with the story of Ray, a teenage party guy who hasn't grown up and isn't sure he wants to. He's choosing fun now over the future he says he wants. He's heading toward what the authors call "a failure to launch." Why? Because the teen years are like a diving board that, if we land on the right spot, will launch us into our best possible future. If we miss (or don't even jump), we risk never launching. The authors then identify five categories of hard things that, if we do them, promise to deliver high-impact results now and later.

Questions for Discussion and Reflection

1. Do you know a "kidult" like Ray? Describe his or her life. Do you think there's anything that anyone could say to someone like this that would motivate him or her to change direction? If so, what? If not, why not?

2. The authors write, "What each of us will become later in life largely depends on what we become now." Do you agree or disagree? What might a mature adult who knows you well say you are becoming?

3. What are some of the hard things you've already done in your life? What were the results? What did you learn through these experiences?

5 THAT FIRST SCARY STEP

How to do hard things that take you outside your comfort zone

"Life is full of scary things," write Alex and Brett. Most of us can relate! The problem comes when we let fear or discomfort limit what we attempt or dream for our lives. If we're willing to act in spite of fear, risk failure when necessary, and trust God, our lives will change radically for the better. And we'll accomplish more than we ever could have imagined.

Questions for Discussion and Reflection

1. Identify the areas in your life where you try hardest to stay in your "cozy little routines." In each case, what negative outcome are you most afraid of? What very positive outcome might come about if you took that first scary step despite your fears?

2. Why might God be able to accomplish more through us when we act in spite of our weaknesses rather than out of our confidence or strength?

3. "Our story started with a simple step into the unknown," Seth Willard says in this chapter. "But by God's grace our story has only just begun." As you were reading this chapter, did any thoughts come to mind about a step into the unknown you should or could be taking? If so, what is it?

6 RAISING THE BAR
How to do hard things that go beyond what's expected or required

In this chapter the twins explore how phrases like "just do your best" can do more harm than good. Comparisons with how others perform don't help either. Instead, teens need to reject complacency by choosing values like "do what's hard for you" and "pursue excellence, not excuses."

Questions for Discussion and Reflection

1. The Bible says, "The complacency of fools destroys them" (Proverbs 1:32). Do you think it's possible to be popular, smart, and successful and still be complacent and foolish? If so, how?

2. Most teens show above-average abilities in at least one area. According to Alex and Brett, what's the danger of defining ourselves by that one area?

3. "Don't do bad stuff" can easily be the default standard of excellence in church circles. Do you see any problem with that? Talk about it.

7 THE POWER OF COLLABORATION
How to do hard things that are too big for you to do alone

Instead of turning away when an idea seems too big for us, the twins argue, teens should turn to collaboration. The fact is, when we work with a team of like-minded rebelutionaries, we can do together what we could never have done alone. The chapter suggests ten practical things the brothers have learned working with teams.

Questions for Discussion and Reflection

1. Have you ever cared a lot about a project only to drop it because you couldn't do it alone? If so, talk about that. What might have happened differently if you'd had a team around you to help accomplish that goal?

2. Alex and Brett talk about how important it is for teens to "walk with the wise." What do they mean by this principle, and why does it matter?

3. As you were reading this chapter, did a "too big for just me" but important goal come to mind? How could you act on that thought or desire? (Hint: Begin with the first thing the authors learned about teams: start with questions.)

8 SMALL HARD THINGS
How to do hard things that don't pay off immediately

Many long-term successes are built on life skills that come from doing small hard things—self-discipline, honesty, consistency, thoughtfulness—and doing them repeatedly over a long period of time. The authors point to the Vikings as an example of powerful sailors who nearly always defeated their enemies in battle. Their success was partly due to one simple fact: they rowed their own boats into battle.

Questions for Discussion and Reflection

1. Have you ever felt like Joanna—"ready and moti-vated to tackle something big and exciting but stuck against your will in a seemingly endless round of chores"? If so, talk about it. Why do you think small hard things can be so hard for teens?

2. What are the small hard things you struggle with most? Describe some of the self-talk that goes on in your head that makes doing those tasks even harder.

3. How could doing everything for God's glory (see 1 Corinthians 10:31) radically influence how you think about and complete small hard things?

9 TAKING A STAND
How to do hard things that go against the crowd

Following the crowd can lead us far astray. In this chapter Alex and Brett talk about why going against cultural norms is a challenge every rebelutionary will eventually face. Then they suggest six principles to help teens "stand at the right time, for the right thing, and for the right reasons."

Questions for Discussion and Reflection

1. When Eva decided to live for Christ, she had to make choices that isolated her from her friends. Have you ever had a similar experience? If so, talk about it.

2. Do you think it's harder to take a stand for what's right around friends who say they are Christians or around friends who don't? What are some of the different challenges in each case?

3. Is there a stand you know you should be taking but haven't? What are you willing to do about it, starting now?

10 GENERATION RISING
Creating a counterculture from scratch
(and a dash of salt)

Now that the authors have described the Rebelution at a personal level, they take the discussion global. What would happen, they ask, if rebelutionaries saw a world-sized need and acted? What would happen if the Rebelution became a counterculture that transformed a generation? Alex and Brett look to two simple but profound word pictures to show what that God-honoring movement might look like: salt and light. Jesus said His followers are both. As salt, we fight corruption and preserve good. As light, we shine truth where lies hold people in darkness.

Questions for Discussion and Reflection

1. Conner Cress's normal life got turned upside down one day when he encountered pictures of hungry,

hopeless children. Have you ever had a similar experience that changed how you saw the world? If so, talk about it.

2. On pages 176–79, Alex and Brett talk about how we need character, competence, and collaboration to truly succeed in our endeavor. Do you agree? Which pillar comes hardest for you, and why?

3. If you were to identify one passion as your "holy ambition," what would it be? Do others know about it? If so, do you feel supported by them? How could knowing your holy ambition help you make decisions and set priorities in the months and years ahead?

11 A THOUSAND YOUNG HEROES
Stories of new beginnings, impossible challenges, and the teens who are living them

"Throughout this book we've asked what it would look like for our generation to start living out the principles of the Rebelution," write the authors. "The truth is that in many ways it's already happening." As evidence, they introduce readers to young people like Zach Hunter, Jazzy Dytes, Brittany Lewin, Leslie and Lauren Reavely, Brantley Gunn, and Leeland Mooring. Each is an "unlikely hero" of the Rebelution—and proof that every teen who desires to follow Christ can be part of this movement.

Questions for Discussion and Reflection

1. Which of the stories in this chapter meant the most to you personally? Why?

2. In telling Zach's story, the guys write: "Zach had found a cause that was bigger than his fear." What is the biggest fear that is keeping you from becoming a change maker for Christ? Where do you think that fear comes from? What does it tell you about yourself?

3. In nearly all the stories in this chapter, the "unlikely heroes" simply said "Yes, God" to a need or an opportunity that was right in front of them. Do you sense God showing you a similar need or opportunity? If so, what is it? How do you plan to respond?

12 WORLD, MEET YOUR REBELUTIONARIES

Transforming your mission from a decision into a destiny

In this closing chapter, Alex and Brett review the main ideas they've covered. Now that the reader has a clear view of a new way of life, they offer some practical advice to get "from big idea to meaningful change." They introduce three typical teens—Noah, Serena, and Brandon—and offer problem-solving ideas for how they can get past their distractions and obstacles. One more story is yet to be told: "And that story is yours."

Questions for Discussion and Reflection

1. Which part of this book inspired you the most?
    Which part made you the most uncomfortable?
    Explain why.

2. Working from the five-step rebelutionary action
    plans that the authors share for Noah, Serena, and
    Brandon (pages 214–24), what is your action plan
    to deal with the distractions and obstacles you face?
    Get help from friends, family, and other advisers as
    needed to create the smartest plan possible. Write it
    down. Then keep your five-step plan where you can
    read and review it every day.

3. Mentally, travel forward one year in your life. What
    do you hope will be different? Five years forward,
    what's your answer to the same question? How can
    the ideas in this book help you get there?

NOTES

Chapter 2

Dawn Eden, "Think big! HS twins tell peers," *New York Daily News*, 28 August 2005, www.nydailynews.com/archives/news/big-hs-twins-peers-article-1.607964.

John Ehinger, "Judicial-Race Excesses," *The Huntsville Times*, 3 October 2007.

Chapter 3

Friedrich Heer, *Challenge of Youth* (Tuscaloosa, AL: University of Alabama Press, 1974), 128, emphasis added.

John Taylor Gatto, *The Underground History of American Education* (Oxford, NY: Oxford Village Press, 2000), 23–24, 30–33.

David Barnhart and Allan Metcalf, *America in So Many Words* (Boston: Houghton Mifflin, 1997), 233–4.

Asa Hilliard III, "Do We Have the Will to Educate All Children?" *Educational Leadership* 49, no. 1 (September 1991): 31–36, quoted in Linda Lumsden, "Expectations for Students," *ERIC Digest* 116 (July 1997).

Denise Witmer, "Teach Teens Responsibility by Setting Expectations," About.com,http://parentingteens.about.com/od/agesandstages/a/responsibility.htm.

Chapter 4

Christian Smith and Melinda Lundquist Denton, *Soul Searching* (New York: Oxford University Press, 2005), 98–99.

J. C. Ryle, *Thoughts for Young Men* (Amityville, NY: Calvary Press, 1996), 10.

Lev Grossman, "Grow Up? Not So Fast," *Time,* 16 January 2005, www.time.com/time/magazine/article/0,9171,1018089,00 .html.

John Piper, *Roots of Endurance* (Wheaton, IL: Crossway, 2002), 126.

Maria Puente, "George Washington cuts a fine figure," *USA Today,* 12 October 2006, www.usatoday.com/travel/destinations/2006-10-12-mount-vernon_x.htm.

Chapter 5

Stanley H. Frodsham, *Smith Wigglesworth: Apostle of Faith* (Spring field, MO: Gospel: 1993).

Chapter 6

Bits & Pieces, 28 May 1992, 15; see also http://net.bible.org/illustra tion.php?topic=294, select "c," then "complacency."

Charles Haddon Spurgeon, *The Treasury of David,* vol. 1 (Grand Rapids: Guardian, 1976), 10, www.spurgeon.org/treasury/ps001 .htm.

Edmund Morris, *The Rise of Theodore Roosevelt* (New York: Modern Library, 2001), 32–33.

Chapter 8

Martin Luther King Jr., "What Is Your Life's Blueprint?" (lecture,
     Barratt Junior High School, Philadelphia, 26 October 1967), as
     quoted at SeattleTimes.com, http://seattletimes.nwsource.com/
     special/mlk/king/words/blueprint.html.

Chapter 10

"Francis Schaeffer, Address at the University of Notre Dame, April
     1981," quoted in Nancy Pearcey, *Total Truth: Liberating Christian-
     ity from Its Cultural Captivity* (Wheaton, IL: Crossway, 2004),
     opening page.

John Piper, "Holy Ambition: To Preach Where Christ Has Not Been
     Named" (sermon, 27 August 2006), www.desiringgod.org/Re
     sourceLibrary/Sermons/ByDate/2006/1790_Holy_Ambition_
     To_Preach_Where_Christ_Has_Not_Been_Named.

Chapter 11

Zach Hunter, *Be the Change* (Grand Rapids: Zondervan, 2007).

Jeremy V. Jones, "End Slavery Now," *Breakaway,* March 2007, 18–22.

Cornelia Seigneur, "Teens open their hearts to Portland's homeless,"
     The Oregonian, 9 August 2007.

Sarah Corrigan, "Brantley Gunn: World-Changer," *Breakaway,* July
     2007.

ACKNOWLEDGMENTS

T o Apple for the MacBook Pro and the iPod Nano.

To Dawn Eden for befriending two inexperienced teen bloggers and encouraging us to keep at it. That meant the world to us.

To the original rebelutionary bloggers who helped launch the movement in 2005: Tim Sweetman, Alex King, Jake Smith, David Ketter, Kristin Braun, Chloe Anderson, Travis Henry, Karen Kovaka, David MacMillan III, Cody Herche, and Marshall Sherman.

To Justice Tom Parker for modeling wisdom, integrity, and humility as a jurist, and for taking a risk by allowing two young men to shoulder real responsibility.

To the staff attorneys at the court for believing with us that sixteen-years-olds can do hard things and for mentoring us through the internship.

To Rebekah Guzman, who lifted our spirits with her enthusiasm and support in the early days of book proposals and tough decisions. And to her husband, Ben. We'll never forget the games of miniature golf, spades, and find-the-German-restaurant.

To Fred Stoeker for all the book advice and writing tips. To Shannon Ethridge for being a prayer warrior and for taking our proposal to Multnomah.

To Steve Cobb, Dudley Delffs, and Ken Peterson at Water-Brook Multnomah. Thanks for believing in a book by two inexperienced first-time authors. To Kevin Loechl for reviewing the contract.

To our editor, David Kopp. You believed in this project way back in March 2006 and kept pushing to make it happen. You're the best of the best. Thanks for helping us take the book to the next level. To Heather Kopp for helping us break down the wall of over-familiarity and find the hidden structure in our rough draft. This book would not have happened without you. Thanks for all the incredible memos.

To Cheri Colburn for heroic line-editing. Your input and polish did wonders. To Julia Wallace and Laura Wright for managing the final details. Thanks for making sure all our t's were dotted and our i's were crossed.

To Alice Crider, Brian Thomasson, and Jessica Lacy in Multnomah editorial. To Joel Kneedler and Melissa Sturgis in publicity. To Tiffany Lauer, Ginia Hairston, Allison O'Hara, and Amy Haddock in marketing. To Carie Freimuth, Lori Addicott, and Steve Reed in sales. To Kristopher Orr and Mark Ford in graphic design. To everyone else at WaterBrook Multnomah whose names we don't know. It was your excitement that was the deciding factor in our decision to write this book with Multnomah. We couldn't be happier with our team.

To Jane Rohman, John Bianco, Nicole Devin, and Molly

Hamaker for their tremendous work as freelance publicists for the book. We're amazed by what you do.

To Evie Schmitt for handling hundreds of e-mails and freeing us up to write. Thanks for the "It's the Book, Stupid" posters. Classic!

To Paul and Jennifer Hartung for the photo on the back cover. You two are like magicians behind the lens. Thanks for making it fun.

To the Menucha Retreat Center and all its staff for being like a second home during key stretches of the writing process. To Phyllis Thiemann for opening Brickhaven Bed and Breakfast to us and for feeding us lunch.

To the teens whose inspiring stories we couldn't fit into the book: Chloe and Petra Anderson, Carly Deburgh, Anna Lofgren, Jordan Schaefer, Kaytlynn Clemons, Chris Field, Haley Allen, Felicity Shepherd, Claire Halbur, Betsy Olson, Charity Edwards, Elisabeth Rifeser, Matthew Champlin, Chelsea Rankin, Adrienne Gilbert, Rebecca Moon, Elisabeth and Kirsten Gruber, Naomi Van Calster, Cornelia van Oostrum, Garret Boon, Martha Heimsoth, Chelsea Convis, Heather Gundlach, Josh Donegani, Katy Owens, Elizabeth Probasco, Naomi Nelson, Caleb Rivera, Sydney Lubin, Victoria Cuneo, Rachel Ramm, and Samantha Loftus, to name a few. A big thank you to all of you. Your stories energized us to finish the race.

To our stellar Forum Team on TheRebelution.com who held down the fort while we were out writing. A big thanks to Mark Hutchins, Jonathan Field, David Boskovic, Alex Poythress, Nathan Sleadd, Hannah Farver, JoAnna Talbott, Kristin Braun, Daniel Osborne, Lindsey Wagstaffe, Isaac MacMillen, Elisabeth Thomas, Brittany Cronin, Tim Heaton, Irene Lee, Rebekah Shinabarger, Beth Magnuson, Stephanie Olsen, Holly Donahue, Carl Gray, Ryan Farrington, Kierstyn Paulino, Abigail Snyder, Heidi Mull, and Nicole Hearn.

To all the rebelutionaries online and at our conferences who prayed for and believed in this project. You are the movement. Keep pressing onward and upward.

To Daniel and Peter Fender for helping to make the writing process more than just writing. Thanks for taking the time to seek the Lord with us, pray for us, and encourage us in our walk with Him. You inspire us.

To our entire church family at Household of Faith. You've watched us grow and seen our many faults. Thanks for your faithful prayers, support, and counsel.

To C. J. Mahaney, Steve Whitacre, Mark Dever, and Jeff Purswell for your steadfast commitment to the gospel. Thank you for your timely exhortation and for communicating your concerns to us with both hope and love.

To Randy Alcorn for everything. You invested countless hours guiding us through every critical step of the publishing process and kept us focused on eternity. You always made yourself available, despite your countless other obligations.

Your counsel and support was invaluable. You went above and beyond. We can't give you enough credit.

To our incredible younger siblings for freeing us to focus on the book and picking up the slack inside and outside the home. Sarah, we've watched our little princess grow up into a caring and capable young woman. Thanks for doing all the important things, big and small, to help make everything we've done possible. You're a gem. Isaac, your faithful service to the family and to us is a blessing. Thanks for being our right-hand man on all our projects. James, your faithful and earnest prayers put us over the hump, buddy. Thanks for giving us all the love in your seven-year-old heart and for all the shoulder rubs and big hugs.

To big brother Joel and wife Kimberly for cheering us on from the beginning and for jumping into the editing process to give helpful input. Thanks for being such faithful counselors and friends.

To big brother Josh. Thanks for taking the time for long phone calls whenever we needed to talk. We'll always look up to you as an author and a man of God. Your investment in our lives through your example and counsel has been challenging to us as brothers and inspiring to us as young men.

To our parents, Gregg and Sono Harris. Your commitment to wisdom, hard work, and the Word of God forms the bedrock of how you have raised your children and how you have directly impacted hundreds of thousands of others. Dad and Mom, your investment into this book was huge. Thanks for staying up late into the night to finish edits before deadlines, neglecting your to-do lists to meet our needs, and for faithfully pointing us to the Cross. Mom, thanks for always caring more about our souls than our success. Dad, so much of this book is informed by the ideas you've been teaching since before we were born. We can't wait for your next book.

To our Lord and Savior, Jesus Christ. This book is for You and only because of You. Time and time again we have watched You orchestrate events in ways beyond what we could have ever imagined. We deserve Your wrath—and yet You freely give us grace.

Soli Deo Gloria!

FREE VIDEO RESOURCE

We partnered with LifeChurch.tv Open to create a four-part series of short videos presenting the "do hard things" message for small groups, youth groups, and churches. We are thrilled with the results. LifeChurch.tv did a terrific job.

The series includes videos on topics such as "The Myth of Adolescence," "Unlikely Heroes," "The Launching Pad," and "Do Hard Things." Each video is five to seven minutes long—perfect for introducing people to the ideas of the Rebelution.

The curriculum also features suggested opening and closing remarks for group leaders, along with small-group discussion guides for each segment. The best part, though? The series and resources are completely free for anyone to download and use. You can find "Fabulous Life of a Teenager—Youth" here: https://open.church/resources/1448-fabulous-life-of-a-teenager.

ABOUT THE AUTHORS

Alex and Brett Harris founded TheRebelution.com at sixteen years old and wrote their first book, *Do Hard Things: A Teenage Rebellion Against Low Expectations*, three years later. They published their second book, *Start Here: Doing Hard Things Right Where You Are*, as sophomores at Patrick Henry College in Virginia. Today they describe themselves as plodding visionaries—intent on making much of their Savior Jesus Christ through a lifetime of faithful service. Alex, married to Courtney, is attending Harvard Law School, following God's call on his life to make a positive difference in the arenas of law and public policy. Brett, married to Ana, is pursuing further ministry through writing.

To get in touch with Alex and Brett, "like" their page on Facebook (Facebook.com/dohardthings), follow them on Twitter (Twitter.com/therebelution), or check out their blog (TheRebelution.com/blog). They'd love to connect with you, hear your stories, and get your feedback.

ARE YOU READY FOR THE NEXT STEP?

Do Hard Things inspired thousands of young people around the world to make the most of the teen years. Now Alex and Brett Harris are back and ready to tackle the questions that *Do Hard Things* inspired: "How do I get started? What do I do when I get discouraged? What's the best way to inspire others?" Filled with stories and insights from Alex, Brett, and other real-life rebelutionaries, *Start Here* is a powerful and practical guide to doing hard things, right where you are. Don't let the momentum fade. Start today.

THE REBELUTION

1 TIMOTHY 4:12

Counter Complacency • Combat Cultural Lies • Change the World

- **Hear from Alex & Brett Harris as well as guest bloggers**

- **Connect with like-minded young people**

- **Find video and downloadable resources**

- **Stay up-to-date with Rebelution activity**

TheRebelution.com